SKETCHBOOK TRAVELER

JAMES LANCEL McELHINNEY

SKETCHBOOK TRAVELER

Southwest

SCHIFFER PUBLISHING
4880 Lower Valley Road • Atglen, PA 19310

Other Schiffer Books by the Author:
Sketchbook Traveler: Hudson Valley, ISBN 978-0-7643-6042-8

Other Schiffer Books on Related Subjects:
Painting the Elements: Air Water Earth Fire, Parramon, ISBN 978-0-7643-5953-8
White! Light! Bright! How to Make Your Backgrounds Support and Enhance Your Watercolor Paintings, Bivenne Staiger, ISBN 978-0-7643-6266-8

Library of Congress Control Number: 2021948651

Cover and interior design by Ashley Millhouse
Type set in Agenda / Chronicle Text
ISBN: 978-0-7643-6325-2
Printed in India

Published by Schiffer Publishing, Ltd.
4880 Lower Valley Road
Atglen, PA 19310
Phone: (610) 593-1777; Fax: (610) 593-2002
E-mail: Info@schifferbooks.com
Web: www.schifferbooks.com

CONTENTS

INTRODUCTION

> The moment I saw the brilliant, proud morning shine high up over the deserts of Santa Fe, something stood still in my soul, and I started to attend.
>
> —D. H. Lawrence (1885–1930)

In Tony Hillerman's slim compendium *The Spell of New Mexico*, D. H. Lawrence lamented how modern transportation distances us from nature, observing that "our great-grandfathers, who never went anywhere, in actuality had more experience of the world than we have, who have seen everything."

Between 1922 and 1925, Lawrence and his wife paid several visits to New Mexico. In 1924, their friend and patron made them a gift of a small ranch twenty miles north of Taos. Passing away during a sojourn in Venice in 1930, Lawrence, or what was left of him, was exhumed and shipped to Marseille for cremation. The plan was for his widow's boyfriend to deliver the ashes to the New Mexico ranch, where Frieda von Richtofen Lawrence (1879–1956) was preparing to build a memorial to her late husband. Dodging customs and red tape, the courier later confessed to dumping the remains into the Mediterranean before crossing the Atlantic. Frieda went to her grave never suspecting that the ashes enshrined at the ranch might have belonged to somebody she never met. Another story claims that Frieda did receive Lawrence's ashes, but she mixed them into the wet concrete used to create his memorial.

The property today is owned and operated by the University of New Mexico. During her first visit to Taos in 1929, Georgia O'Keeffe claims to have lain supine on Lawrence's writing bench. Gazing heavenward from beneath the spreading branches of the large ponderosa pine inspired her to devote a canvas to *The Lawrence Tree*, completed the same year. Of the tree, Lawrence wrote, "One goes out of the door and the tree-trunk is there, like a guardian angel."

During our last visit to the ranch, Kathie Manthorne and I found the large wire-fence gate locked with a stout chain. Upon close inspection, I discovered it was a ruse. The padlock dangled from one link. The remainder of the chain had been deceptively wrapped around the gate's pipe frame. As we swung open the gates, the caretaker rolled up in a pickup truck. We followed him up to the house.

After trudging up the path to visit Lorenzo's monument, we headed back to the garden. Taking turns lying on the bench, we gazed up through the branches of the great tree, as O'Keeffe and many others had done. Performing this ritual felt like kissing the Blarney Stone or rubbing the nose of the Bowling Green Bull, except that we were partaking in an experience that had sparked creativity in others.

Driving downhill through a pine forest, we reached the valley below. Spreading out to the north, south, and west, punctuated by ancient cinder cones and volcanic uplifts like Ute Mountain, the broad plain was broken by the distant serpentine gash of Rio Grande Gorge. Somehow, in the unknowable vastness of the American Southwest, ordinary rocks and trees seem to gather around them unbidden powers that offer protection one minute and peril the next. Its ungovernable spaces inspire awe, invite meditation, and summon visions.

Many years ago, hiking along the edge of Tsankawi Mesa, it occurred to me that were I to lose my footing and plunge to my death, it might take days or even weeks to find the body, unless Raven and Coyote had already made a feast of my corpse and scattered its bones. In a landscape bereft of physical sustenance, only spirits can dwell. Gazing east from the rim across Buckman Mesa I beheld the warm earth, submerged in cool shadows. Above the deepening gloom, Sangre de Cristo mountains arose, awash in the ruddy glow of sunset. Alighting on a bushy pinyon beside me, a talkative crow kept me company at nightfall, as a swarm of stars filled the heavens. How unlike being alone in the wild, on the edge of a precipice, is solitude of each point of light, adrift in an infinite universe? Hovering below the mountains, off to the southwest, the electric glow of Santa Fe shattered my reverie. Heading back to the parking area, I backtracked through rocks and scrub across the mesa. Flying from one treetop to another, my corvid companion shadowed my footsteps back to the car.

My first visit to New Mexico was in the late 1970s, in the company of a dear friend whom I would later marry. Our union did not last, but my love affair with the Southwest has endured. Having grown up in the Delaware Valley in southeastern Pennsylvania, I was keenly aware of a tradition of artists' colonies in Bucks County and the Brandywine Valley. Members of the Wyeth family of Chadds Ford established beachheads in both Maine and New Mexico. Pennsylvania native John Sloan made several trips to the Southwest, as did Marsden Hartley, John Marin, Stuart Davis, Edward Hopper, Josephine Nivison Hopper, Dorothy Brett, Georgia O'Keeffe, and Agnes Martin. Philadelphia painters such as Tom Palmore and abstract illusionist James Havard relocated to New Mexico, as did other prominent artists including Larry Bell, Ron Davis, Richard Diebenkorn, Bruce Nauman, and Susan Rothenberg. The story goes that more than a century ago, a group of artists moved to Taos, enchanted by the crystal-clear light and gob-smacking scenery. Nicolai Fechin, Ernest Blumenschein, Joseph Henry Sharp, Walter Ufer, Gustave Baumann, Bert Geer Phillips, and Victor Higgins established studios in what had been a sleepy town on the edge of the mountains.

Cultural tourism in the area had been successfully promoted by Fred Harvey (1835–1901), who established a chain of restaurants, hotels, and souvenir shops along the Atchison, Topeka, and Santa Fe Railroad. The Harvey Company staffed its facilities with Harvey Girls, reputable educated white women between the ages of eighteen and thirty. It also escorted passengers on "Indian Detours" to visit pueblos and trading posts where they could purchase Native American weavings, pottery, and jewelry. This planted the seed for Santa Fe becoming one of the four leading art markets in the United States, a position it still holds today. It proved also to be the genesis of the annual markets that specialize in traditional and contemporary arts and crafts by Native American and New Mexico Spanish makers. One of the attractive features of the Southwestern art scene is a causal indifference toward Eurocentric distinctions between fine art, folk art, and crafts, which seems to reflect the ethnic diversity that characterizes much of the region.

In a nutshell, New Mexican society is divided into three primary groups. Indigenous communities include the more ancient Tewa, Tiwa, and Keresan Puebloans, and the Athabaskan Diné (Navajo) and Apache, who migrated into the area a thousand years ago. The Navajo Nation, which straddles New Mexico, Utah, and Arizona, is the largest indigenous sovereign territory within the United States. Puebloan Hopi lands exist as an administrative island, surrounded by Navajo lands.

Spanish settlers arrived in the late sixteenth century, only to be expelled by a Native revolt in 1680. Returning twelve years later, Spanish conquerors reached an uneasy accord with their hosts, settling colonists on royal land grants that extended north to the Arkansas River.

The opening of the Santa Fe trail, and the outcome of the Mexican-American War of 1846–48 triggered an influx of a non-Native, non-Spanish Anglo population. The term is applied universally to anyone who is neither Native nor Spanish, be they of European, African, or Asian descent.

Part of this book is devoted to Tsé Bii' Ndzisgaii (Valley of the Rocks), better known as Monument Valley, located in the northeast corner of the Diné reservation. This impressive array of red sandstone buttes has become synonymous with the American West, appearing in such films as *The Harvey Girls* (1941), *Easy Rider* (1969), *National Lampoon's Vacation* (1983), *Thelma and Louise* (1991), and *Forrest Gump* (1994). None of these stunning geological formations were visited by nineteenth-century explorers, whose focus was on discovering mineral resources or viable railroad rights of way. John Ford valued it not only as a location for such classic westerns as *Stagecoach* (1939) and *The Searchers* (1956) but also because it was far enough from Hollywood to discourage micromanaging studio executives from pestering the director with unwelcome visits. The fame of Monument Valley has proved to be a mixed blessing to the local Diné, whose revenue has come to depend on tourism by hosting strangers on sacred lands.

Three hours east of Los Angeles, photogenic Joshua Tree National Park and Coachella Valley in southern California have also provided filming locations for *It's a Mad, Mad, Mad, Mad World* (1963), *Tell Them Willie Boy Is Here* (1969), *The Big Year* (2011), and countless television commercials. The arid desolation of the southern Mojave Desert makes New Mexican deserts seem Edenic by comparison. Yet perched at Keys View, overlooking Coachella Valley toward Mount San Jacinto, or south along the ridge of the San Andreas Fault toward the Salton Sea, one is gripped by a sense of awe, a terrible and liberating feeling of profound insignificance. Clinging to the surface of a planet spinning at more than a thousand miles per hour, orbiting the sun at more than nine times the speed of sound, the clustered petals of *Atriplex canescens* tremble gently in a warm breeze. The land itself seems to possess a beating heart, a mind and a purpose.

In his book *The Man Made of Words: Essays, Stories, Passages*, Pulitzer Prize winning author N. Scott Momaday (1934-) observes:

> We look at a given landscape and take possession of it in our blood and brain. For this happens, I am certain, in the ordinary motion of life. None of us lives apart from the land entirely; such an isolation is unimaginable.

The American Southwest has become a magnet for those seeking spiritual renewal, or a place to pursue unconventional lifestyles. Perhaps the region's ethnic and social diversity nurtures a higher degree of tolerance, despite abiding contrasts between these groups in terms of wealth and power. The region today faces an imminent crisis caused by a sharp uptick in population, exerting unsustainable pressure on limited sources of water for drinking and irrigation. History may be repeating itself. Seven hundred years ago, the depletion of resources forced the abandonment of urban and ceremonial centers at Chaco Canyon, triggering a diaspora that established new settlements along the Rio Grande and elsewhere.

No better place can be found for the development of mindful practices than vast expanses of raw terrain. Absent of lush forests, untamed by pastoral cultivation, like the Biblical trope of wilderness, these are the places where one may battle dark forces, commune with the Divine, and discover oneself. Let's return to Tony Hillerman (1925–2008), who recalled, "I have never yet made that long monotonous drive through the great vacancy between Albuquerque and Roswell without finding my head filling with ideas crying to be written." Hillerman's words apply also to drawing, which is nothing more than writing in visual terms.

For inspiration to find us, we must first take action—with the scratch of a pen or the stroke of a brush.

Chapter 1

LA TIERRA INCOGNITA

> All over the land are vast and handsome pastures, with good grass for cattle, and it strikes me the soil would be very fertile were the country inhabited and improved by reasonable people.
>
> —Álvar Núñez de Cabeza de Vaca (ca. 1490–ca. 1560)

In 1536 the residents of Culiacán were met with the strange sight of three Spaniards and one African, clad in Indigenous clothing, emerging from the untamed margins of the settlement. Álvar Núñez de Cabeza de Vaca had been an officer in the doomed expedition led by the one-eyed conquistador Pánfilo de Narváez. Shipwrecked by a hurricane, hounded by hostile Native peoples, and then shipwrecked again on the Texas coast, the survivors built a flotilla of makeshift rafts that was scattered by yet another storm. Enslaved by the local residents of Galveston Island, Don Álvar and his companions proved useful to their captors, who benefitted from the Spaniards' knowledge of medicine and trading acumen. Having become semi-assimilated, they were free to commence an eight-year trek through south Texas and into what is today Coahuila, New Mexico, Arizona, Chihuahua, and Sinaloa. Welcomed both as merchants and healers, Cabeza de Vaca's little band is believed to have traveled as far north as Las Cruces. Some claim they visited the village of Hawikuh, near present-day Zuni Pueblo. Returning to Mexico, they carried out exploits embellished by tales of golden cities and riches beyond measure.

When Francisco Vázquez de Coronado set off to locate them in 1540, all he discovered was a miserable cluster of huts near what is now Lyons, Kansas. In the process, he explored stretches of the Colorado River and established contact with the Puebloan culture of the Rio Grande Valley. Subsequent expeditions brought prospectors, settlers, and ultimately Spanish dominion over land extending as far north as Ohkay Owingeh (San Juan Pueblo) and Taos, until a Native uprising expelled the Europeans for twelve years. When in 1692 the reconquista met with fierce resistance, Spanish and Native authorities came to an understanding that amounted to a symbiotic alliance against hostile raiders living on the fringes of the fertile Rio Grande and its tributaries. In 1848 this multicultural community of Pueblos and Spanish land grants was absorbed into the United States, adding yet another layer of Anglo civilization onto this unique and diverse region.

> We have an unknown distance yet to run, an unknown river to explore. What falls there are, we know not; what rocks beset the channel, we know not; what walls ride over the river, we know not. Ah, well! we may conjecture many things.
>
> —John Wesley Powell (1834–1902)

Prior to the US Civil War, New Mexico extended as far north as the Arkansas River and west to Nevada. The great rivers—Gunnison, Colorado, Arkansas, Canadian, Chama, and Rio Grande del Norte—rise in what is today central and southern Colorado. The Pecos flows out of the eastern slopes of the Sangre de Cristo Mountains, flowing southward to the east of the Rio Grande, until the two rivers meet east of Big Bend, near Comstock, Texas. The Gila River rises on the western slope of the Continental Divide north of Silver City, New Mexico. Fed by rivers like the San Fernando, San Pedro, Santa Cruz, Salt, Verde, Agua Fria, and numerous smaller tributaries, the Gila flows westward across Arizona to its confluence with the Colorado at Yuma. In northern Arizona, the Colorado River system has hewn a spectacular congregation of deep gorges known collectively as the Grand Canyon. The Colorado turns southward, crossing the northwestern margins of the Sonoran Desert before dumping its waters into the Sea of Cortez.

Along its right bank, the Mojave Desert extends hundreds of miles to the north and west, meeting the Sonoran Desert at Joshua Tree, on the heights above the Coachella Valley in Southern California. The San Andreas Fault is visible as a low ridge running from northwest to southeast to the Salton Sea, just north of Palm Springs. The geological character of the region expresses a wondrous, diverse array of tectonic and volcanic activity, augmented by millions of years of erosion from wind and water, carving spires, arches, and canyons. Much of the region stands at high elevations, giving sunlight an almost blinding intensity, while volatile weather patterns can send temperatures soaring or plunging within a short time. The most precious resource in the region is water, the lack of which explains why vast expanses remain uninhabited. In the more verdant zones of New Mexico, a system of ditches, or acequias, has been established, maintained under the feudal control of a ditch boss, or mayordomo. Both New Mexico and Arizona are peppered with Indigenous territories, the largest of which is the Navajo Nation traversing the Four Corners region, encompassing landmarks such as Shiprock, Monument Valley, Chaco Canyon, and Canyon de Chelly.

> Ruins provide the incentive for restoration,
> and for a return to origins.
>
> —John Brinckerhoff Jackson (1909–1996)

Ruins of dwellings constructed by the Athabaskan Diné (Navajo) people and the proto-Puebloan Anasazi dot the terrain. Appealing to early European visitors, these historic remnants of abandoned settlements were revered as cautionary relics of human hubris and as reminders that all human endeavor needs improvement. The first artworks produced in this culturally rich environment were Indigenous petroglyphs, ceramics, basketry, and textiles that displayed symbolic, rather than mimetic, imagery. The first artists trained in the Western tradition to visit these regions accompanied military expeditions and railroad and mineral surveys. These included Richard H. Kern and his brother Edward, who delineated topographical views and maps for John C. Frémont. Drawing in sketchbooks, elaborating their field notes back in the studio, these expeditionary artists provided illustrations for official reports. Conducted between 1848 and 1855, the Mexican Boundary Survey employed such artists as John Russell Bartlett, Henry Cheever Pratt, Arthur C. V. Schott, and Augustus Vaudricourt to depict the terrain, flora, and fauna of newly acquired territories.

In the postbellum period, professional studio artists began to seek inspiration in the American West. Published in 1873 by George Putnam in New York, Eliza Pratt Greatorex's *Summer Etchings in Colorado* was one of the first books by a woman to propose a Grand Tour of trans-Mississippi North America. Hudson River School artists like Albert Bierstadt, John Frederick Kensett, and Worthington Whittredge tramped across the Plains and into the Rockies. Thomas Moran's paintings of Yellowstone and the Grand Canyon helped sell the idea of National Parks to Congress. Working in concert with the Atchison, Topeka and Santa Fe Railroad, Fred Harvey developed a new brand of mobile hospitality, building modern hotels near train stations and running motor tours to bring travelers in contact with Native artists selling jewelry, pottery, and weavings. By the turn of the nineteenth century, artists were moving to Santa Fe and Taos, some for the scenery and brilliant sunlight, others for relief from respiratory ailments offered by the clean mountain air. The artists who formed the core of the Taos Art Colony in the early twentieth century—Ernest L. Blumenschein, Walter Ufer, Victor Higgins, and Maynard Dixon—celebrated the spectacle of nearby mountains and canyons while producing genre scenes of the Puebloan community. Within a few years, artists from New York including John Sloan, Marsden Hartley, and John Marin would make seasonal visits to northern New Mexico. Others who flocked to Taos included Ansel Adams, D. H. Lawrence, and Georgia O'Keeffe, who arrived in 1929. O'Keeffe established a permanent residence at Abiquiu, in the Chama River valley. Agnes Martin moved to New Mexico in 1968. Larry Bell arrived in 1973, Bruce Nauman in 1979, and Ron Davis in 1991. In 1979 Donald Judd's Chinati Foundation acquired much of a decommissioned army base at Marfa, Texas, devoting the space to installations by Judd and his contemporaries. For many years the landscape painter Rackstraw Downes has wintered along the Rio Grande near Big Bend.

With its museums, galleries, opera, and ethnic markets, Santa Fe has long been reputed to possess one of the most vibrant artistic communities in the United States. The Southwest continues to attract artists, hikers, anglers, and sports enthusiasts to test their mettle against the rugged conditions of a still-forbidding wilderness. In places where mortal peril attends every step in the form of violent weather, wildlife, rock falls, and avalanches, one is naturally inclined toward mindfulness.

> Artwork is a representation of our devotion to life.
>
> —Agnes Martin (1912–2004)

Confronting the Sublime teaches us to respect and revere nature. In many ways, the West is America. With its breathtaking terrain, enchanting beauty, and aggregate culture, few places are more American than the Southwest. Having once experienced it, some part of it remains with us wherever else we may go. Such is its beauty, power, and allure.

> I have found a dream of beauty at which one might look all one's life and sigh.
>
> —Isabella Lucy Bird (1831–1904)

Chapter 2

LA TIERRA ENCANTADA

In the magnificent fierce morning of New Mexico, one sprang awake, a new part of the soul woke up suddenly, and the old world gave way to a new.

—D. H. Lawrence (1885–1930)

Reckoning all my separate visits to the Southwest over the years, I have spent years exploring its rivers and mountains, historic sites, and byways. The only direction from which I have yet to approach the region is from the south. Most historic trade routes and itineraries followed by historic expeditions have been leveled, banked, and paved for automotive use. One exception is Medano Pass, where Zebulon Pike led his party over the mountains, north of Blanca Peak in southern Colorado. Those who have yet to visit the region might be taken aback by the weather. Contrary to Hollywood visions of sunny days and golden mesas, one may wake up to snow, playing golf after breakfast and skiing in the afternoon. The high desert and mountainous regions receive heavy snowfall in winter and blistering heat in summer.

My first trip to the Grand Canyon was during a blizzard. Elevation seems to be a determining factor. The south rim of the Grand Canyon stands at nearly seven thousand feet. The north rim is almost two thousand feet higher. El Paso sits at 3,740 while Los Alamos is at 7,320. Traversed by the San Andreas Fault, the Coachella Valley is more than twenty-five hundred feet below nearby Joshua Tree National Park. Stretching fifty miles south, the valley descends more than two hundred feet to the Salton Sea. The Southwest is a land of extremes. Its varied climate may be attributed to the combined forces of volcanism and plate tectonics that have shaped the terrain, watered largely by snowmelt in the high country. The playwright Arthur Miller told a story about flying over the basin-and-range country west of the Rockies. Seated next to him was a geologist who claimed that one of the largest aquifers in the world lay a mile below the desert. If it could be tapped, the man explained, the arid zone below could be transformed into productive farmland. Miller asked him how it could be done. With atom bombs, he was told. Miller asked, "Wouldn't that contaminate the water?" "That's not my department," the geologist replied.

Vast areas of the Southwest are uninhabited because they are uninhabitable, chiefly due to the lack of surface water for cultivation. Spanish settlers dammed waterways and dug acequias—small irrigation canals—to carry water from streams and rivers into their fields. Cultivating hardy indigenous species of squash, pumpkin, maize, and chili peppers, colonial farmers were able to sustain a modest population settled along streams, rivers, and flood plains. Their agrarian know-how was enhanced by local practices. No other part of the United States has such a large and visible Native population. Apart from the Tewa, Tiwa, and Keres pueblos scattered up and down the Rio Grande, there are the Athabaskan Diné (Navajo) and the traditionally nomadic Jicarilla, Mescalero, and Chiricahua Apache scattered between west Texas and Arizona. The need for protection from invaders and marauders led to the construction of Tyuonyi pueblo in Frijoles Canyon and Tsankawi, both in Bandelier National Park near Los Alamos. The Navajo Nation commands sixteen million acres, comparable in size to West Virginia. Native American communities have all run afoul of Euro-American conquerors. Only the Puebloans managed to expel the Spanish in 1680 for a dozen years, resist conquest in 1692, and come to an understanding with the outsiders that have helped them preserve their religion, culture, and language to the present day. Leapfrogging Native settlements, Spanish land grants colonized the area. Developing a symbiotic rapport and some degree of tolerance, Spaniard and Indian formed alliances for mutual defense against bloody raids by their nomadic Athabaskan neighbors.

Puebloans had long been master potters and weavers. Blending cultures led to the rise of new artistic traditions in the form of distinctive silverwork, textiles, and ceramics. Traditional Indigenous mural arts had been limited to petroglyphs and wall paintings, but under Spanish influence hybrids began to emerge as naïve iterations of Churrigueresco chapels and altars in Catholic churches that stand in the plazas of Spanish villages and beside Native kivas. While Native towns like Taos, Acoma, and Zuni have survived down the centuries, many more have been abandoned. Apart from the ruins of quasi-urban settlements at Chaco Canyon and Mesa Verde, one finds remnants of hardscrabble villages deep in the cañadas or on mesa tops. Ruins appeal to a romantic Euro-American appetite for the picturesque. Relics of human endeavor, they abide as durable reminders of its ephemeral nature. Ruins provided expeditionary artists with geometric pictorial devices that served as markers of antiquity comparable to the great Mississippian mounds at Cahokia, Teotihuacán in central Mexico, and Troy at Hissarlik.

My first visit to Chaco Culture National Historical Park was in the dead of winter. Approaching the site from NM Highway 44, we turned left onto an Indian service road. Soon the pavement gave way to gravel and then to mud. Blanketing the desert overnight, a considerable snowfall was beginning to melt, turning the road surface into slippery, gelatinous mush. Our Toyota pickup fishtailed its way through a ribbon of brown slush. Passing a collapsed Hogan and a rusted-out car peppered with bullet holes, we saw in the distance another vehicle heading our way. Like the Navajos in the other pickup, we sat three abreast on a bench seat. We slid one way, their vehicle slid the other. Like ballroom dancers, we passed within an inch of collision. Screaming like kids on a roller coaster, we parted without incident.

As impressed as I was with the architecture, the most durable takeaway for me was a cautionary tale about reckless stewardship of natural resources. The site of Chaco was established along the green banks of a flowing stream. Over the centuries, the inhabitants had denuded the surrounding plain of its forests, farmed the land to exhaustion, and finally set different factions within the community against one another. Many traveled east to the fertile Rio Grande valley. Others headed south and west. One band is believed to have been the forerunners of the founders of Tenochtitlan. When I mentioned that I had seen fragments of Chacoan pottery atop a mesa near Los Alamos, a ceramist at Santa Clara quietly shared that while elders shun talk of Chaco, everyone knows its tragic backstory.

During my first painting trip to New Mexico, wherever I unpacked my gear and got to work, a crow would arrive. Sitting on a piñon branch, the bird kibitzed until I packed up and left. Days passed. Imagining it was the same bird that was keeping me company, I dubbed him Don Juan in honor of Castaneda's Yaqui brujo. Crows are notoriously intelligent, cunning thieves, equal to the ubiquitous magpie. Call it a departure from reason. Perhaps I had just surrendered to the fact that regardless of what passed for normal back East, here all deals were off.

> Elsewhere the sky is the roof of the world; but here the earth was the floor of the sky.
>
> —Willa Cather (1873–1947)

Tierra encantada is also tierra embrujada—haunted land. In the twilight desolation of a mesa top, the presence of spirits, angels, and shapeshifters seemed possible. Beneath a canopy of stars, one has the sense of standing atop a living thing with a mind, a soul, and a beating heart. This notion of a living earth has made the Southwest a magnet for devotees of New Age spirituality. Blending modern crime drama with Native mysticism, Tony Hillerman's popular mystery novels delve into Diné religious belief. The ethnographer Frank Hamilton Cushing lived as part of the Zuni community from 1879 to 1884. His books and articles helped to illuminate Puebloan life, culture, and spirituality. Frank Waters's *Book of the Hopi* appeared at a time when many of my peers had become disillusioned with the American Dream. Disheartened by the ongoing conflict in Vietnam, many opted for alternative lifestyles. Books by Edward Abbey and Carlos Castaneda were on every counterculture bookshelf.

While many recent Latinx immigrants follow Evangelical ministries, many descendants of Spanish land-grant families remain committed to Roman Catholicism. Deep in the mountains and in some remote areas, Penitente churches can be found where congregants welcome physical ordeal as a form of worship. Elsewhere, most are content with a conventional mass. The Sanctuary at Chimayo attracts hundreds of thousands each year. In a small office by the door, a priest welcomes visitors and comforts the afflicted. In a side room to the left of the altar is the pocito sagrada, or little well of holy dirt, believed to possess healing powers. Abandoned canes, crutches, and other relics of infirmity line the long, dimly lit gallery leading outdoors.

Raised never to discuss religion or politics in polite company, I might add water rights to that list when visiting New Mexico. The American Southwest is a thirsty land that depends heavily on springtime snowmelt and seasonal rainfall. Acequias are communal waterways divided into administrative districts, each with its own mayordomo. Disputes can erupt into lengthy feuds, such as in John Nichols's novel *The Milagro Beanfield War*. Other environmental worries include waste management and toxic runoff from mining and industry. Los Alamos Nuclear Laboratory periodically vents its reactors, releasing radioactive vapor into the atmosphere. Carbon emissions from Los Angeles, Las Vegas, Phoenix, and Albuquerque contribute to spectacular sunsets by fouling the air with greenhouse gasses.

> In the clear blue atmosphere of this elevated plateau, every object appeared with great distinctness, so that mountains could be seen at a distance of more than a hundred miles.
>
> —John Russell Bartlett (1805–1886)

Population growth has increased the strain on natural resources in ways that are unsustainable. In an attempt to dissuade miners from prospecting in Colorado's Boulder Valley, Chief Niwot of the

Southern Cheyenne nation predicted, "People seeing the beauty of this valley will want to stay, and their staying will be the undoing of the beauty." Considering the disastrous history of Chaco, one wonders if history might repeat itself. How can it be delayed or prevented? Artists were the first to depict many of these natural wonders. Let them be first to preserve them. The first step is to promote environmental awareness. This book is an attempt to send people out into nature and have them respond to their experiences by picking up a pencil or a brush. Reviving the spirit of expeditionary art requires us to strive beyond the pleasures of plein-air painting by preparing for outdoor adventures and getting acquainted with our subjects before we head into the field. The more that we, like our historic predecessors, know the history of a place, the more mindful we will be of its people and culture. Likewise, the better our understanding of its geology, climate, and natural history, the more thoroughly we can comprehend what we behold. The goal is not to produce works of art but to deepen our connection to the world around us in ways that transform experience into knowledge and ideas.

Chapter 3

LESSONS IN PRINT

> But it is certain that the common practice of modern landscape-painters is against me. The most of them combine the occupation of the artist with the amusement of the tourist. Turner was a great tourist, especially on foot, and much in the habit of slight and rapid sketching, as is convenient for traveling artists. Now for the tourist sketcher, who travels rapidly, a tent at all heavier than a colorman's sketching-tent is a useless encumbrance. A mere sketcher can get to an inn at night, and I should never recommend him to adopt a tent as a habitation . . . let him live at the inns. Or, if he is a good walker, a knapsack, sketching-block, and stout stick, with two good pairs of boots, and a little money in his pocket is all he needs.
>
> —Philip Gilbert Hamerton (1834–1894)

Hamerton never visited the American Southwest, but his words should resonate with any traveling artist. Pause, take notes, let subjects take you by surprise. Slow down. On your way to bucket-list destinations, you might miss what could later become personal favorites. Landscape painters refer to their subjects as "motifs"—opportune arrangements of topography, weather, and foliage that suggest a composition. Seeking out motifs is like prospecting for gold. A telltale twinkle in a pan full of wet silt tells us to unpack the mule and get to work. When I am working in my journal, a slight turn of the head can reveal an even better subject. The landscape is not what we behold but how we inscribe our desires upon the terrain.

> Landscapes do not occur in nature, but are created when humans adapt terrain to their use.
>
> —John Brinckerhoff Jackson (1909–1996)

When planning a trip, identify your destination. Estimate the duration of your visit and the travel time required. Acquaint yourself with maps, travel guides for your destination, and field guides to wildlife, plants, and geology. Know the history of your destination and its region. Create an equipment checklist. Make sure to pack everything you will need. Check the weather prior to departure. Make appropriate adjustments of supplies, clothing, and equipment. Identify an emergency contact. Let them know your travel plans. Carry their contact information on your person. Travel with a companion or just go it alone. Once on site, follow your plan but be prepared to improvise. Should you get off the beaten path, keep track of your location. Know what time the sun will set, and keep an eye on the clock. Set aside one to three hours at each stop to take in your surroundings, to write and draw. Take your time. Savor the journey. Carry in, carry out. Leave everything you encounter just as you found it.

MAPPING AND COMPOSITION

> In drawing there is only the straight line and the curve Line. Everyone can draw a straight line, everyone can draw a curve line, therefore everyone can draw.
>
> —Thomas Gimbrede (1781–1832), drawing master, US Military Academy at West Point, 1818–32

Composing a picture is the pictorial equivalent of making a map. During the eighteenth century, topographical artists like Thomas Davies and Paul Sandby developed a kind of picture making that dovetailed seamlessly with cartography. Cadets at Woolwich and later West Point received artistic instruction. It was believed that topographical artists trained to produce works of military and scientific value would become keener observers in the field by also pursuing aesthetic goals. Let's explore a few mapping concepts that will help us get going.

THE FRAME

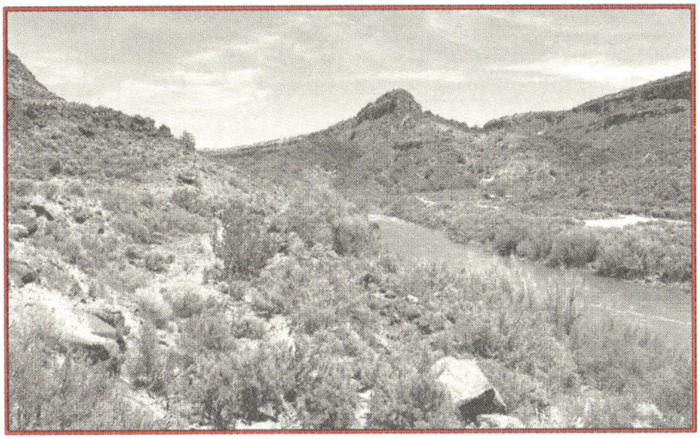

Actors learn how to walk across a stage. Painters must also own their space. To begin, let's use a photograph I took from behind the western bank of the Rio Grande. First, draw a rectangle, or use the boundaries of the page as your frame. Because this book is written for a general readership, I will approach the process of laying out a picture as though we were looking through a camera's viewfinder. One of the first mistakes beginners make is to look at what they are trying to draw, forgetting that the biggest thing in the drawing is the frame itself.

THE HORIZON

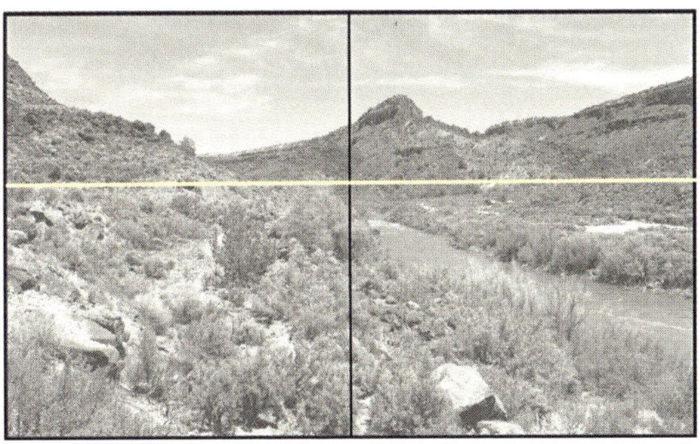

Locate the horizon. This represents your eye level, the boundary between what is up and what is down, as seen from your perspective.

Use the sketchbook's gutter—the gap between the pages—as a device to establish the direction of your line of sight. Take out a compass. Note the degrees and direction from your position. If you have access to cellular service, take out your phone. Open your map app. Find your position on the map. Note the temperature and the weather. This action may not improve your drawing technique, but knowing where you are might help you be more mindful of other things.

QUADRANTS

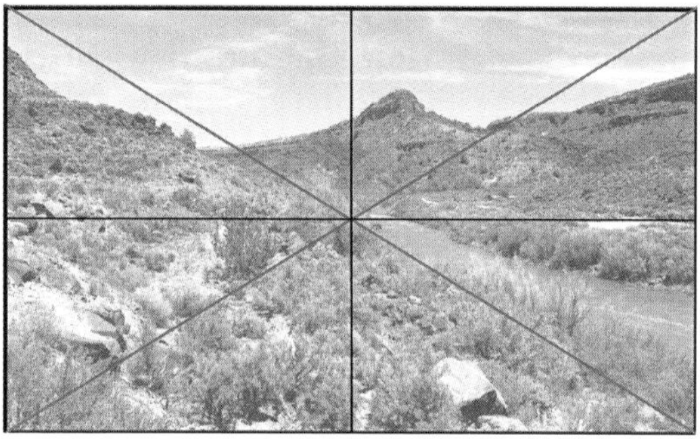

Locate the center of the frame. In an open sketchbook, the top and the bottom of the frame will be represented by the head and the foot of each page. The fore edges define the left and the right sides of the frame. Connect opposing corners by drawing two diagonal lines across the frame. Where these diagonals intersect will be the center. Draw a horizontal line through the center point to the opposing fore edges. Together with the gutter of the book, this line divides the frame into quarters, or quadrants: four rectangles equal in size and proportion to the overall frame. If you are working on a single sheet and not in a sketchbook, you will have to draw a vertical line when you draw the horizontal.

PRIME FOCAL POINT

Look at each quadrant. Which of the four seems most complete as a composition in its own right? That is where you might wisely locate

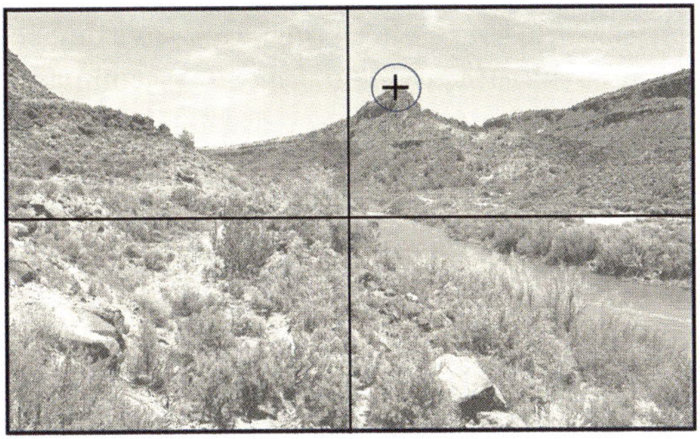

your prime focal point. Your line of sight is the direction you are facing. Your prime focal point is what first catches your eye. In this image, that would probably be the rocky butte located slightly right of center. Of the four quadrants, it is the only one that has a foreground, middle ground, and distance. In the bottom left-hand corner we see the river and its left bank. Rising above it there is the rocky butte, and beyond we behold the distant rim of a canyon wall. Our composition will be anchored on this quadrant, setting the pace for the rest of the image.

THE RULE OF THIRDS

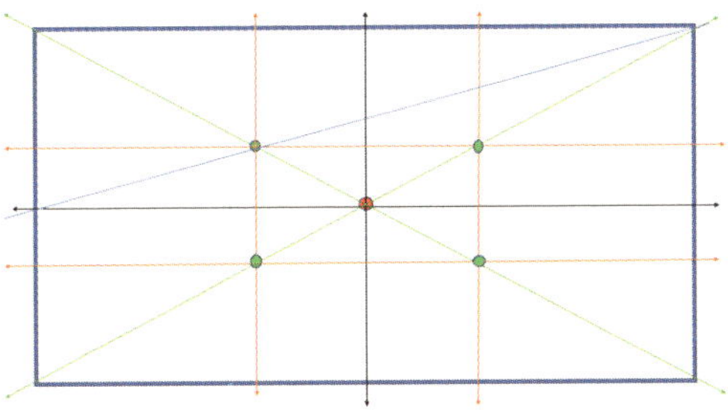

The preceding lesson gives us one way to avoid falling into the common trap of putting our prime focal point in the center of the page. Another way is to use the Rule of Thirds. Once the frame has been divided into quadrants, draw a blue diagonal line from the midpoint of either the left or the right side, connecting to the opposite corner. Note the point where it crosses the green diagonals, connecting opposite corners of the frame. Next, draw a red vertical line and a red horizontal line through the point. Note the point where these lines cross the opposing diagonals. Repeat the process using these new points to locate the fourth point. The purpose of these four green points is to deflect our attention from the red center point of the page and to remind us of the four corners of the frame.

APPLYING THE RULE OF THIRDS

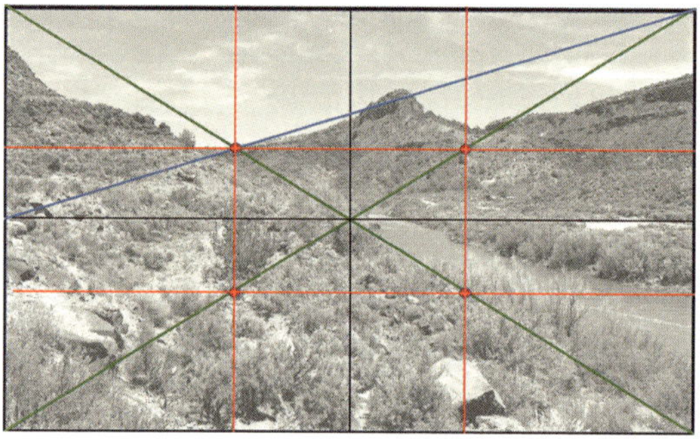

Note the position of the four points we just plotted in relation to features and landmarks within the terrain. That will help locate them accurately in your drawing or painting.

METES AND BOUNDS

One of the fundamental concepts devised for optical surveying is metes and bounds: a system of land measurement based on triangulation. A baseline is established between two known positions. Sighting a landmark from these positions yields different compass headings. Not only would trigonometry provide the distance from baseline to object, but it would also determine the area enclosed within the triangle, according to whatever standard of measure was required.

Applying this concept to drawing is much simpler. Note a landmark you wish to locate within the frame. Using a straightedge such as a

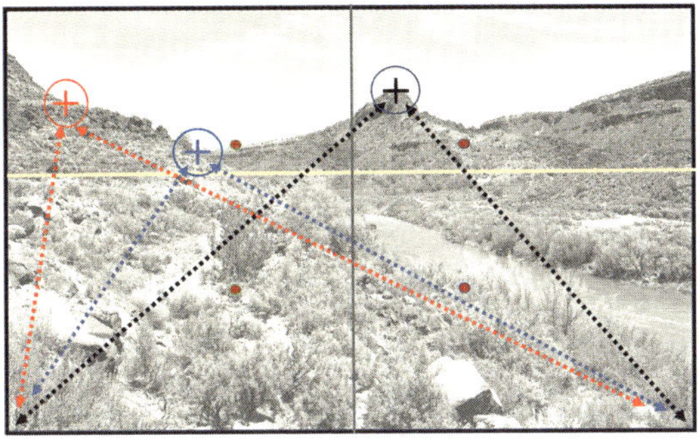

pencil or a kebab skewer, determine the alignment between the object (such as the rocky butte) and the bottom left and right corners of the frame. You can check your work by using the same method to plot the point from any side of the frame. Although it is potentially tedious, one could lay out an entire drawing this way by repeating the process for every object and landmark and then connecting the dots.

GENERAL ALIGNMENTS

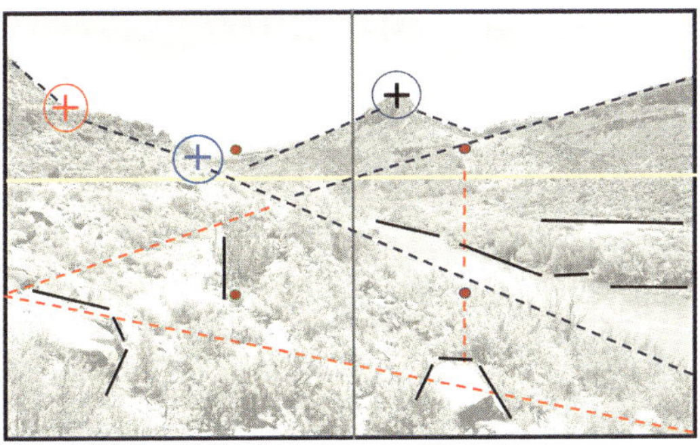

Once you have determined the location of key landmarks, use the same method to map the angles of features, such as the angle of an escarpment receding into the distance. Note how the near edge of the riverbank aligns with the sloping rock fall to the left, creating a line that carries our eye into the space. Notice how the angle represented by the rim of the distant canyon points to the boulder in the lower left-hand corner. Connecting the point at which this angle meets the left edge of the frame with the lower right-hand corner plots a line through another large rock in the foreground. That rock is also vertically aligned with the two right-hand points in the Rule of Thirds and the notch where the slope below the rocky butte crosses the downward angle of the distant canyon rim. Thinking in this manner will help you avoid the pitfalls of mimetic rendering. Copying shapes gets in the way of understanding form and space.

HIDDEN ABSTRACTIONS

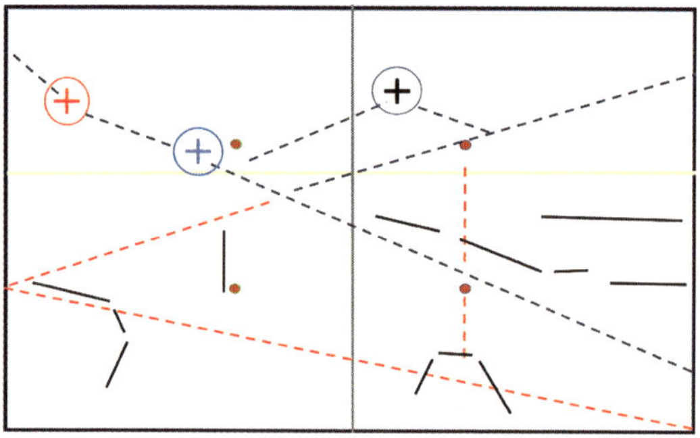

The California painter Frank Galuszka once observed that a good representational painting is easier to produce than a good abstract painting. The conundrum is that within every representational painting there exists an abstraction—its composition. Making a diagram of Cézanne's *Boy in a Red Waistcoat*, the Abstract Expressionist painter Knox Martin declared, "This is art." Composition is the music within every painting. As with life drawing, one must locate the bones and musculature before describing flesh, likeness, or expression.

MAPPING THE IMAGE

Sketching lightly, try to discover movements in the topography, for example the terrain rising to a hilltop or the course of a river or a stream. Your goal is to draw the space, not individual rocks, trees, or clouds. Go back and again use vectors to check your measurements.

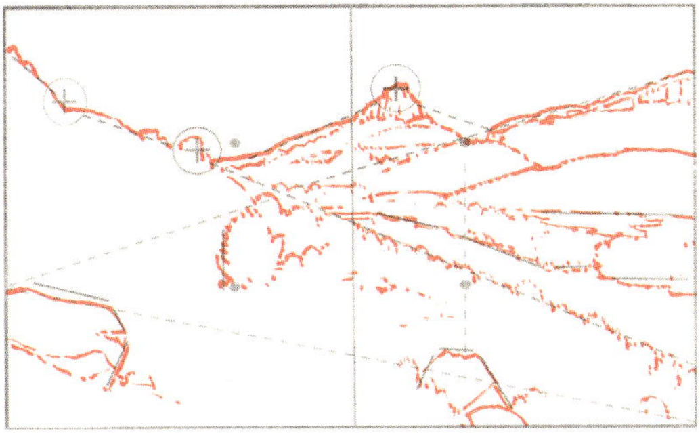

You can follow this method for the smallest detail. Always begin your drawing with the largest forms, never with the specifics. When we first look at a sweeping vista, we see the space and then the major landmarks; then slowly, over time, we discover the details. It's only natural to unpack a drawing in precisely the same way. Once you feel comfortable with this process and have gained confidence in rapid sketching, you might take notes with a pen or a brush in black and white. Using a pencil lets you correct, but in experiential drawing there are no mistakes, only decisions. If you prefer the feeling of drawing with a pencil, do not use an eraser. Write down what you behold in real time, as you take notice of one thing and then another. Think of the page like a tablet or a mode of transmission. The only drawings that matter are those inscribed onto your mental hard drive. They teach you what you behold. When you know something, you will be able to draw it. It's about the process, not the product.

A drawing is an experience made visible. When approaching drawing as a holistic practice, composition reigns supreme. Novices and acolytes in certain cults of virtuosity place a premium on the perfection of descriptive technique. A well-organized composition will always make up for a clumsily rendered form. Since design is more logical and thus simpler to teach than studio magic tricks, a rudimentary grasp is far more accessible. There is no such thing as a bad drawing—only good drawings and research.

The first step in producing a good result is to organize a solid, legible composition. Composition is easily understood in theory, but

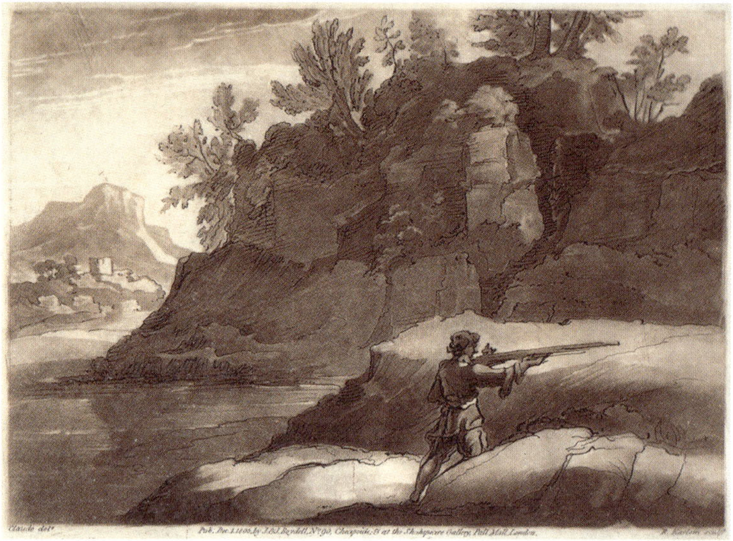

Claude Lorrain, *Liber Veritatis*, Plate 26. Etching with mezzotint on paper. Private collection.

mastering it could take a lifetime. The best way to learn about pictorial composition is by copying masterworks—not with the aim of reproducing them but, like a forensic anthropologist, to analyze their working parts. Let's take a look at two historic compositions.

Claude Gellée, called Le Lorrain (1600-1682), was first among painters to copyright his images by gathering two hundred original compositions in his *Liber Veritatis* (Book of Truth), which was later published in England as a series of etchings. Claude's compositions inspired landscape painters as well as topographical and military artists to seek more poetic results. The practice of paying attention to how visual data fit together sharpened one's powers of observation; the same applied to the field practice of American expeditionary artists such as John Russell Bartlett, Seth Eastman, Edward and Richard H. Kern, H. Balduin Möllhausen, and John Mix Stanley.

Born in Prussia, Heinrich Balduin Möllhausen (1825–1905) came to America to find work in the booming market for picturesque prints of America's natural wonders. English artists such as William and Thomas Birch and Joshua Shaw, the Irishman William Guy Wall, and the French naturalist Jacques-Gerard Milbert flocked to the United States to profit from the popular demand for scenic imagery. Few of these artists were academy trained, but most had been schooled in the military-topographical tradition that flowered in Europe during the mid-eighteenth century. Liberties were taken to privilege certain features of terrain; things that most photography at the time would be hard pressed to capture. This lithograph is based on a sketch that Möllhausen produced while accompanying the US Topographical Engineers expedition exploring a route for the Pacific Railroad along the 35th Parallel. This image was published in the expedition's official report.

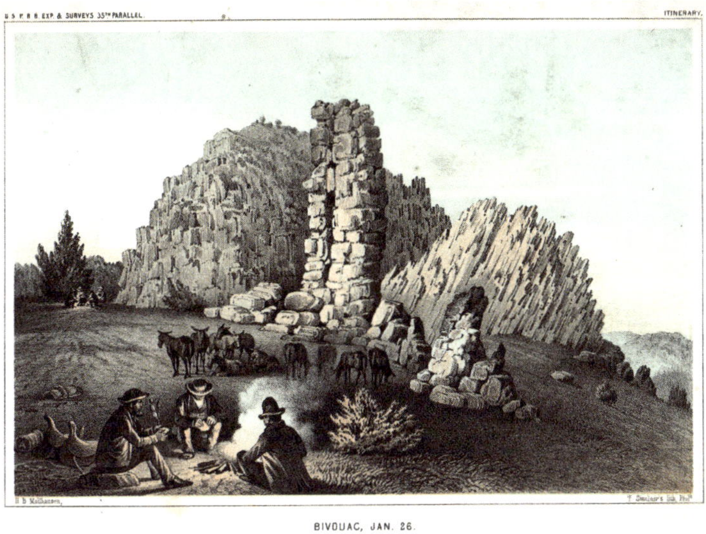

H. B. Möllhausen, *The Bivouac, Jan. 26*, ca . 1855. Hand-embellished three-color lithograph on paper. Private collection.

Do not feel pressured to finish a painting in the field if it just doesn't happen. A complete idea can be formed without completing a painting. By the same token, a finished painting does not necessarily represent a complete idea. Take notes until you have gathered enough data to unzip the file back at your campground, hotel room, or the comfort of home. Consult your own photographs; don't copy them. Use them to help you remember what you drew. Photography was still in its infancy when the unlucky Dick Kern was killed by a Paiute war party in Utah. Less than twenty years later, the former painter William Henry Jackson traveled with Thomas Moran as part of F. V. Hayden's mineral survey of the Yellowstone Caldera. Moran filled his notebooks with drawings and watercolors but was not shy about consulting photographs for factual information.

> We made several photos which will give me all the details I want if I conclude to paint the view.
>
> —Thomas Moran (1837–1926)

Landscape and nature photographers will find that journal drawing and painting in plein air will expand and enrich their own practice. Drawing will not only improve your photography; it will also enhance the pleasures of travel by inviting you to slow down in the presence of nature. Whether in an elegant bistro or at the rim of a wild canyon, a sketchbook can become your home away from home—an office in your pocket. Notwithstanding the pleasures of plein air painting, expeditionary journaling provides us with a nimble mobile practice that can increase the benefits of travel by making our experiences more memorable.

Chapter 4

GALLERY IN PRINT: JOURNAL PAGES

The artworks in this chapter include a range of visual materials to provide a more complete overview of fast-paced fieldwork. The aim is to promote a mindful cognitive practice that will deepen your engagement with nature in ways that transform experience into knowledge and ideas. the point is to move beyond the challenge of producing a finished painting in the conventional sense. Beginning in the nineteenth century, landscape painting migrated away from the notion of finish in favor of a more experiential notion of completeness. By rendering every detail, topographical artists of the eighteenth century sought to develop a pictorial equivalent of cartography. Understanding that light and weather never hold a pose, artists like J. M. W. Turner and Paul Cézanne approached the plein air experience as the pursuit of fleeting sensations. To succeed, one must attempt to move within the flow of time. Given five minutes or five hours, one has enough time to form a complete thought. These thirty images and texts explore three subjects in the vast American Southwest: the Rio Grande Valley in northern New Mexico, Monument Valley in the Navajo Nation, and Joshua Tree National Park in Southern California. This focus allows the reader to explore each location in greater depth.

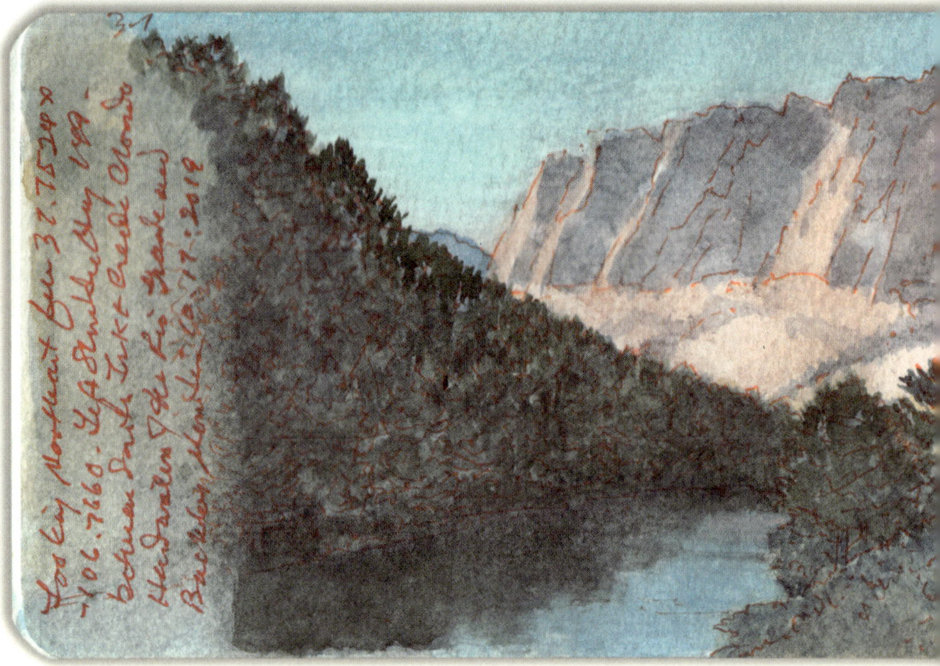

Fig. 1.

BACHELOR MOUNTAIN NEAR CREEDE, COLORADO

North of Del Norte, Colorado, is La Garita Caldera. Its massive eruption during the Cenozoic era dumped vast quantities of ash and debris across the surrounding terrain. Twenty-five million years of erosion have created rocky spires and other picturesque formations within the Wheeler Geological Area, which is managed by the US Forest Service. Similar formations extending to the west include Bachelor Mountain, which rises above the village of Creede, Colorado. During the 1880s, silver mines fueled a booming community and like many mining camps, Creede became a den of iniquity infested by organized crime. Silver mining declined in the wake of the Panic of 1893, but ranching continued in the bottomlands south and west of Creede. Mining survived on lead, zinc, and copper. Today, dude ranches and fly-fishing camps

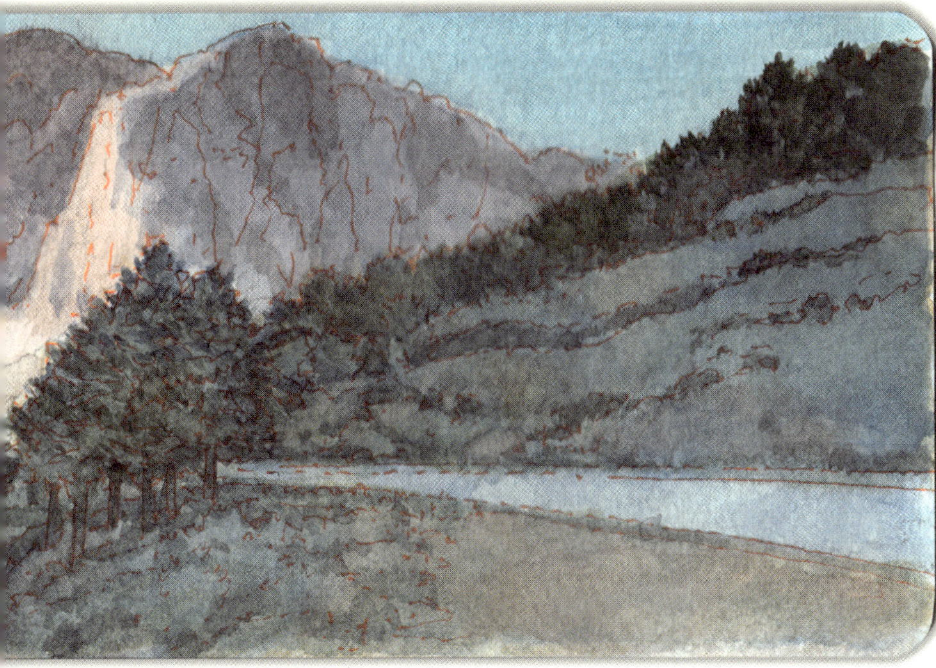

along the headwaters of the Rio Grande contribute to the local economy. Driving north from Del Norte past South Fork, Colorado, Highway 149 ascends the Rio Grande through a deep defile, framing the distant distinctive mass of Bachelor Mountain—an outlier of the Wheeler formations ten miles to the east. If you question why I chose not to hike the ridgeline in search of a better view, the answer is that the first rule of traveling in wilderness areas is never to do it alone. Leaving the car on a wide shoulder above the river, I located this prospect looking northwest from 37.7592 x -106.7813. Framed by high wooded ridges on both sides, Bachelor Mountain is reminiscent of Titian's Dolomites, Thomas Moran's Mount of the Holy Cross, and Cézanne's Mont Sainte-Victoire.

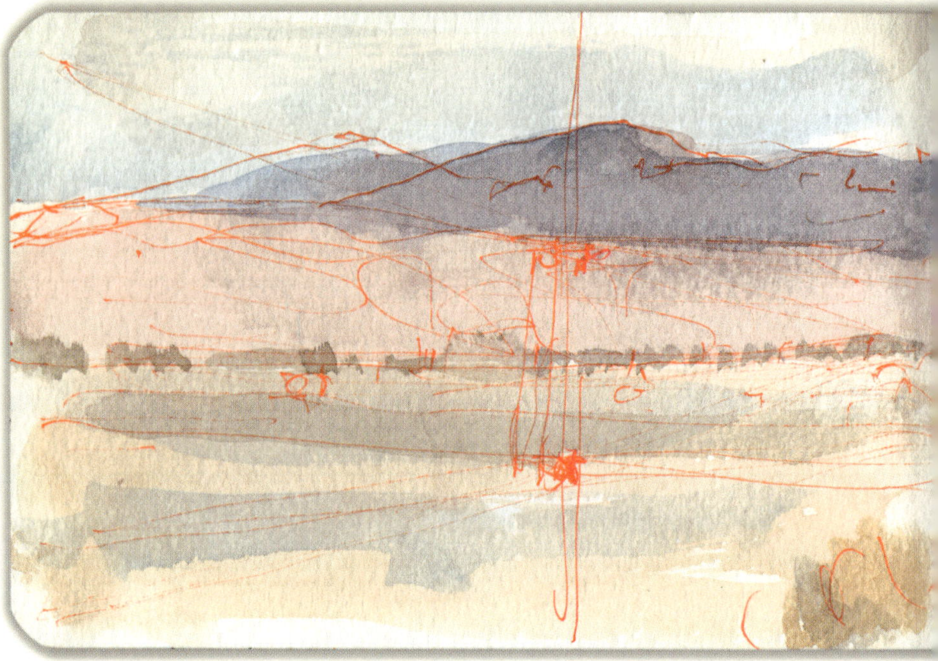

Fig. 2.

LOOKING NORTHWEST ACROSS MEDANO CREEK,

Following the Louisiana Purchase of 1803, the United States extended west into the Rocky Mountains. In 1806 a military expedition led by Lieutenant Zebulon Pike was sent to explore the southernmost reaches of the newly acquired territory. Proceeding west along the Missouri and then north to the Republican River, Pike established contact with Indigenous nations before heading overland to locate the Arkansas River—the southern border with New Spain. Following its course upstream, Pike was greeted by the sight of soaring peaks along the western horizon. Pushing onward into the mountains, the party made a few wrong turns, costing them precious time. Departing the Arkansas, Pike and his band turned south across Wet Valley, then west into broad San Luis Valley over Medano Pass. At the foot of the

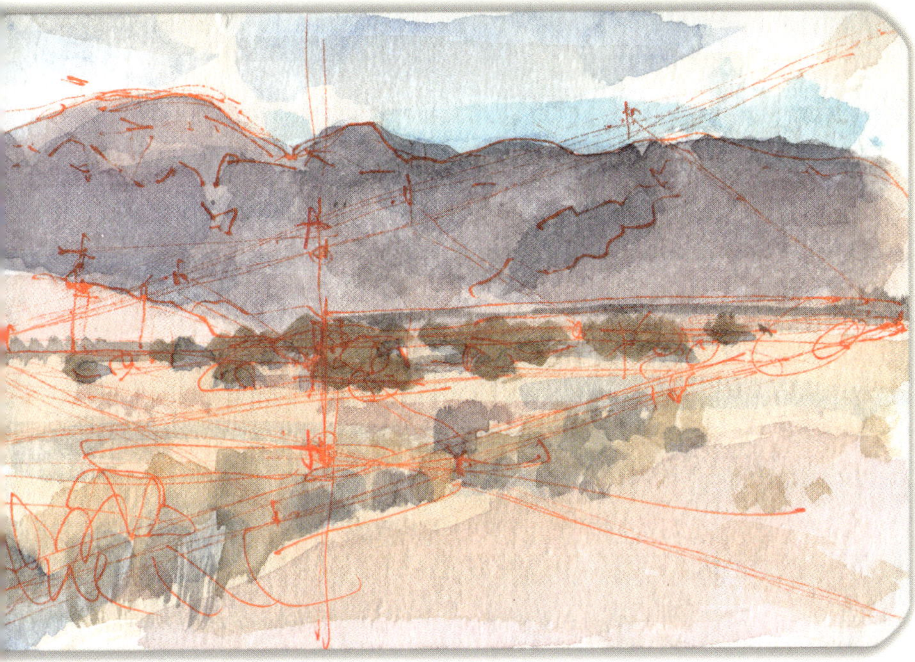

GREAT SAND DUNES NATIONAL PARK, COLORADO

mountains, the men beheld a vast expanse of sand dunes. Covering an area of more than thirty square miles, the sediment of a long-vanished lake had been piled up against the mountains by prevailing westerlies. Pike noted in his report, "We discovered at the foot of the White Mountains which we were then descending, sandy hills. . . . When we encamped, I ascended one of the largest hills of sand, and with my glass could discover a large river. The sand-hills extended up and down the foot of the White Mountains about 15 miles and appeared to be about 5 miles in width. Their appearance was exactly that of the sea in a storm, except as to color."

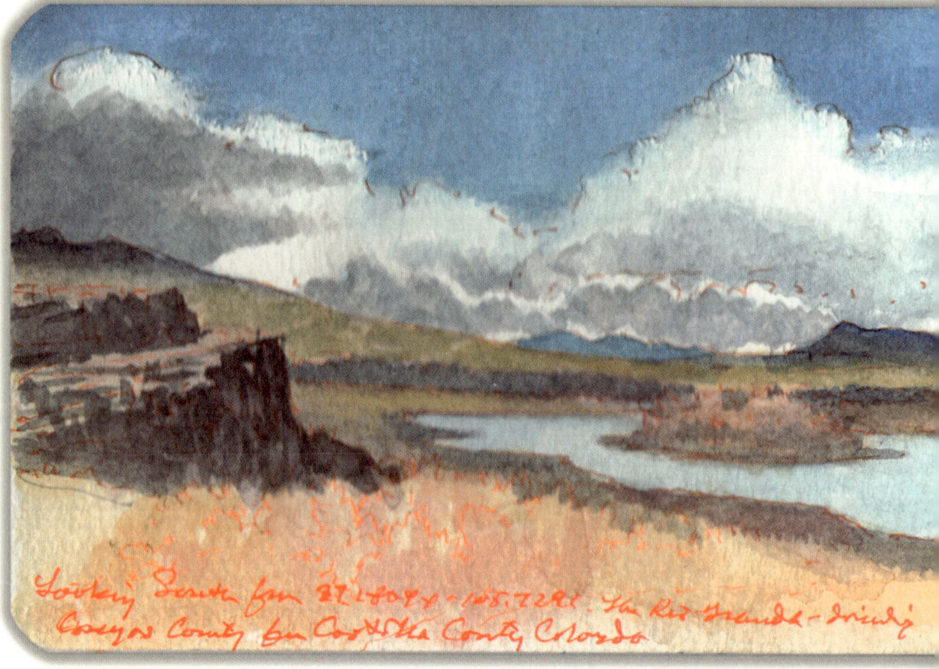

Fig. 3.

CONEJOS-COSTILLA COUNTY LINE

Dividing Conejos County to the west from Costilla County to the east, the Rio Grande traverses the southern margins of the San Luis Basin then descends into a ditch that widens downstream to a quarter mile, reaching depths of more than eight hundred feet. Rising in the San Juan Mountains west of Creede, the river flows east past Alamosa, turning south after the mouth of Rio Conejos (Rabbit River), to meet another tributary—Rio Costilla (Rib River), just north of the Colorado–New Mexico Border. After studying maps over breakfast at the Windsor Hotel in Del Norte, I followed the Rio Grande past Monte Vista to Alamosa, where I turned south onto Highway 285—the road to Santa Fe—passing the village of La Jara, named for Cistaceae, a species of desert flower commonly known as rock-roses. Turning east onto

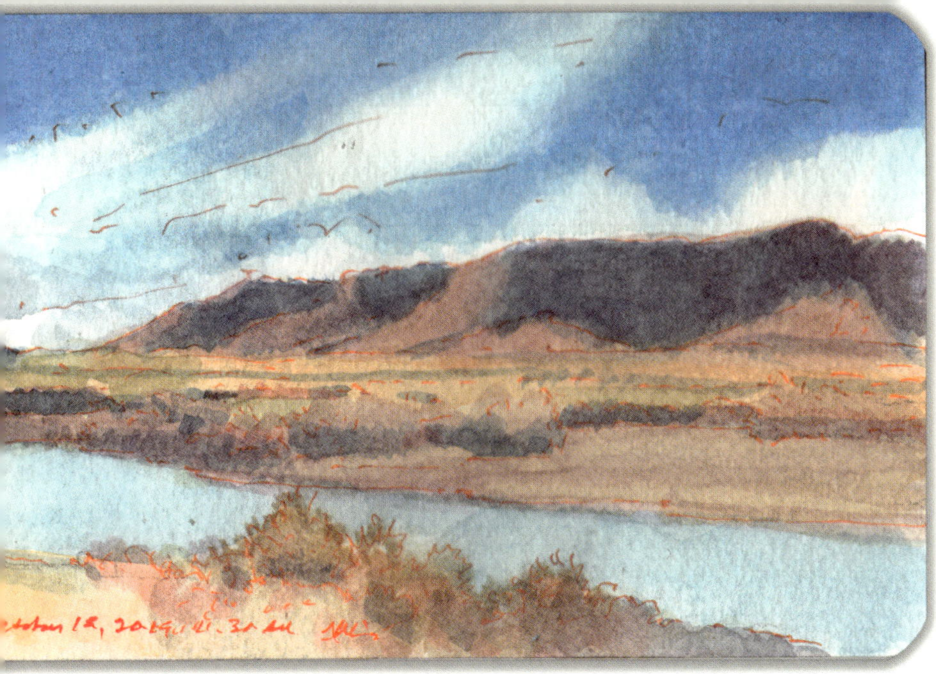

Colorado Highway 142 at Romeo, past Manassa, the road traverses the Conejos River a few miles below its confluence with the Rio Grande. Undulating grasslands spread out across the San Luis valley, supplanted farther south by high-desert sage and piñon. Parking my car on the east bank of the Rio Grande in Costilla County, I walked back across the bridge in search of a compelling visual narrative. Birders from Montreal arrived keen on finding a migratory rarity that had been spotted in the area. Both upstream and down, the waterway was flanked by modest outcroppings worn by erosion. Green tendrils swayed beneath the clear water. I was surprised to learn that the elevation was 8,000 feet.

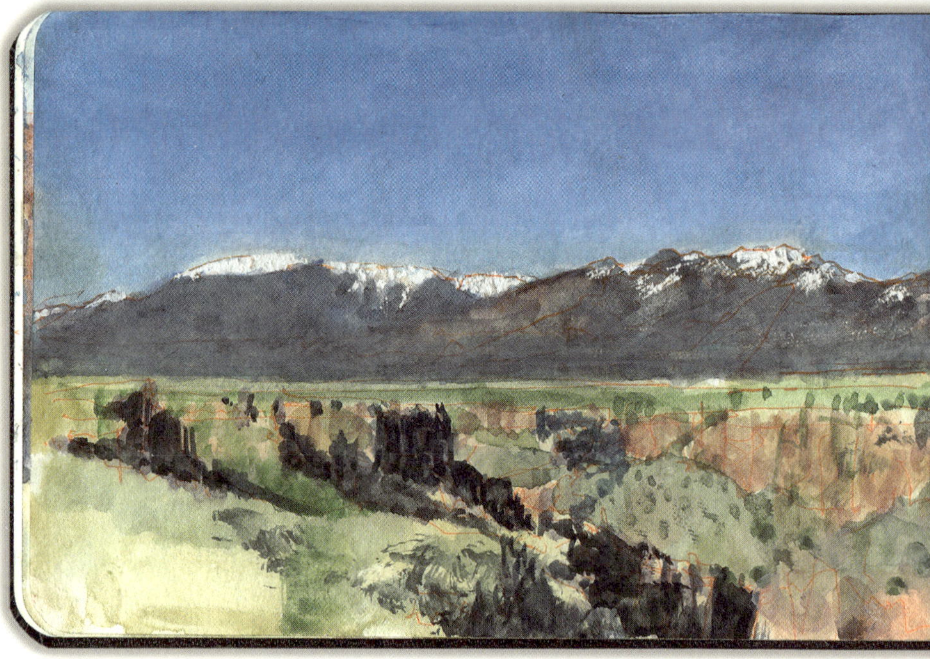

Fig. 4.

RIO GRANDE GORGE BRIDGE

Running between the Llanos Estacado of northwestern New Mexico and Tres Piedras to the west, US Highway 64 crosses a broad volcanic field, reaching from the Sangre de Cristo Mountains in the east to the Tusas range in the west. Situated at the northern end of the Española basin of the Rio Grande Rift, the Taos Plateau is punctuated by extinct volcanic cones and lava domes. The most recent major eruptions were roughly forty thousand years ago. Rising to the surface, geothermal waters have been used by spa resorts from Jemez Hot Springs to Ojo Caliente. Sufficient geothermal activity may exist for it to be harnessed as a renewable source of energy. Taos Plateau is traversed from north to south by the Rio Grande, cutting a deep gorge through more than seven hundred feet of volcanoclastic sediment.

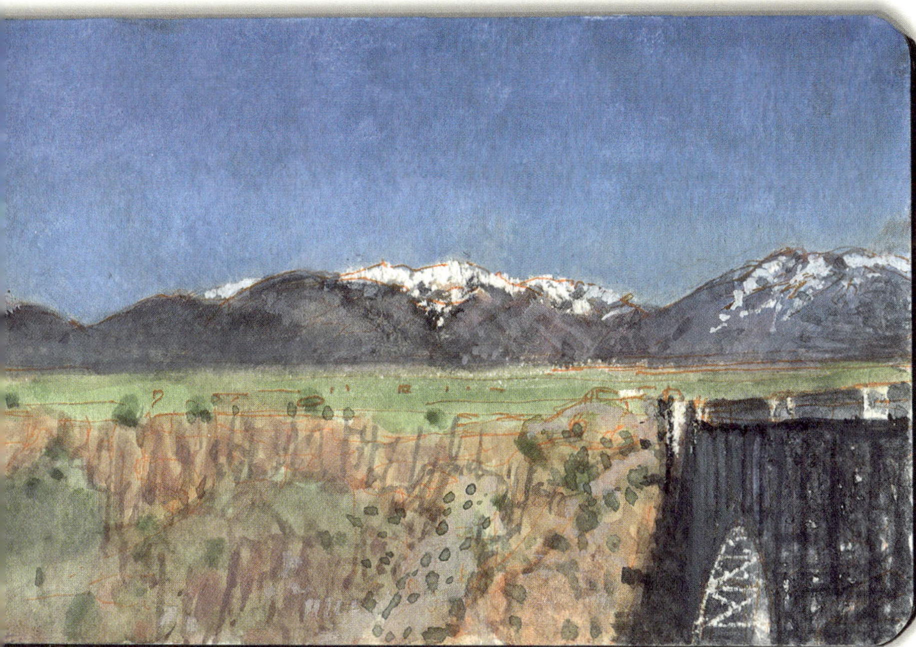

Archaeological evidence indicates a human presence in the region for more than eleven thousand years. Prior to the completion of the High Bridge in 1965, river crossings involved a descent into the gorge via tributaries such as the Red River of New Mexico, Arroyo Hondo, and Rio Pueblo de Taos. Having visited the span on many occasions, I never tire of its vistas. Scorning local ordinances, artisans from Taos Pueblo set up tables on the shoulder of the highway. Turning a blind eye to these vendors on most days, the police might shut them down at any time, just to remind them who is in charge. A day or two later, the little roadside market will be back in business.

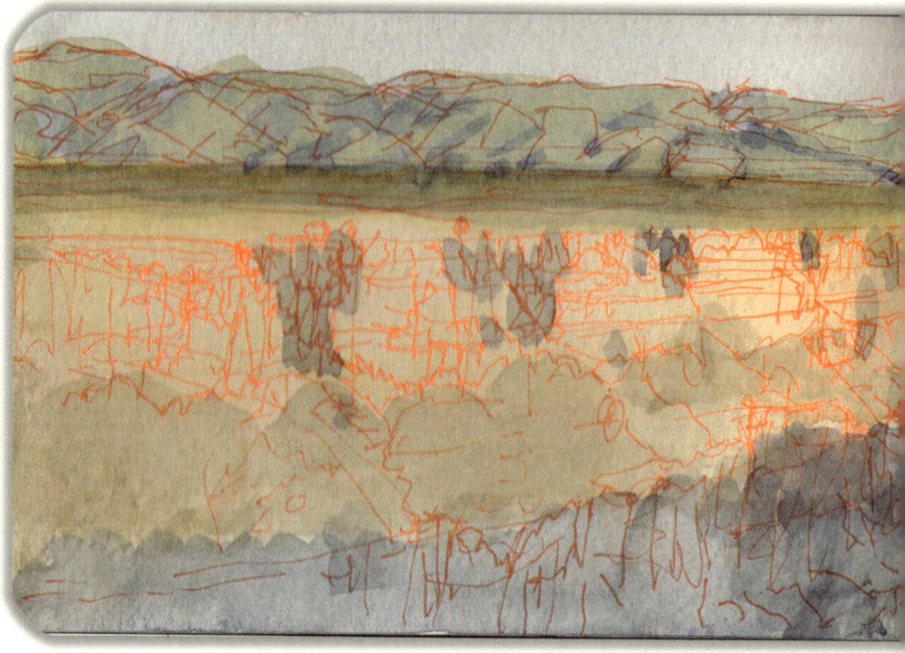

Fig. 5.

LOOKING SOUTH-SOUTHWEST FROM 36.4758, -105.7332

The March day was cold. Snow had fallen overnight. County sheriff's deputies had closed the northern shoulder along Highway 64 at the western bridgehead, forcing Native vendors who usually set up there to move their displays to a paved parking lot off the south side of the road. Having been told to stay off the pavement, they placed their tables on the rocky margins of the high desert. Visiting the little market, I slipped on a slab of black ice and bounced off the ground back onto my feet. A large Taos man named Lujan laughed and asked if I were a stuntman. "No, just lucky," I replied. Heading off down the trail, I wore an Orvis cross-body fishing bag, with a wood-and-leather tripod stool slung over my shoulder. Straying off the trail over toward the rim, I found a rocky corner. Collapsing into a pile of rock fall, a fifty-yard

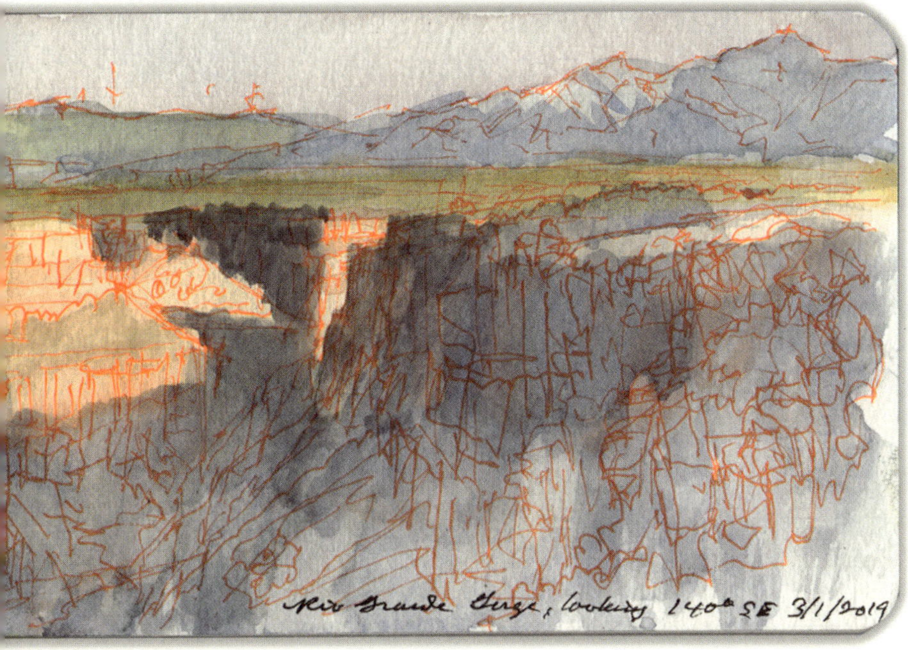

section of the rim rested at a forty-five-degree angle above a sheer drop of perhaps two hundred feet. This widened my view into the canyon and across the Taos Basin toward Picuris Peak. Laying out my composition, I sought to justify alignments between the foreground and the profile of distant mountains. Taking a photograph on my iPhone was useless. Mechanical optics can never replicate the human experience of looking first at one thing and then another. Shadows lengthened. Strong winds arose. After toughing it out for another forty minutes, I returned to an empty parking lot. The vendors had already left.

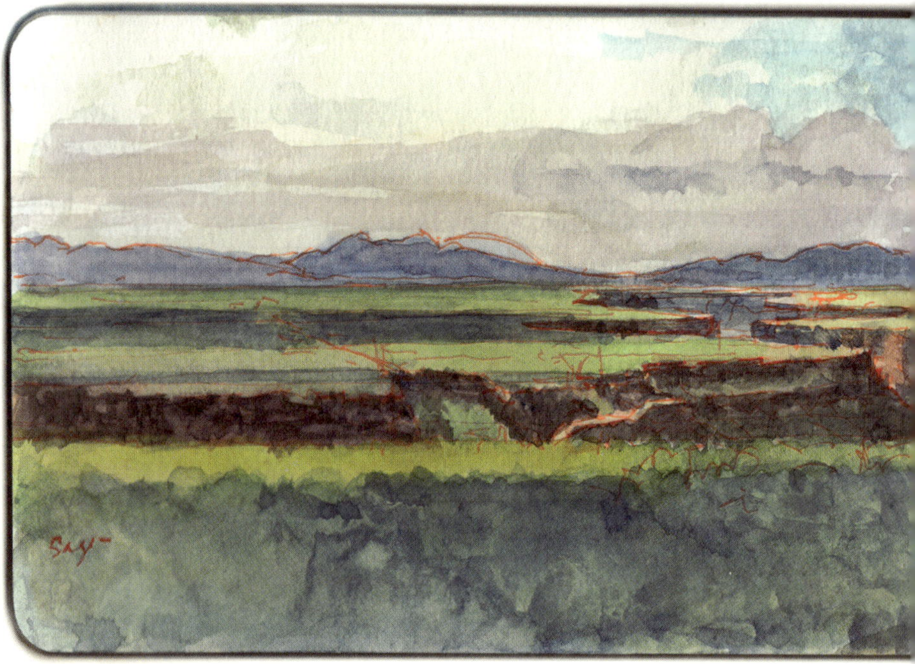

Fig. 6.

ROADSIDE VISTA, RIO GRANDE GORGE FROM NM68,

Two hikers climbed over the wire fence a hundred feet behind me to the south. Motorists pulled over and snapped photos. Nearly all of them held their phone or camera aloft, arms fully extended, as if they could peer into a thousand-foot ditch two miles away. Speeding past, drivers honked and waved at me. Taos Valley is the southernmost extremity of the San Luis basin, which marks the northern end of the Rio Grande Rift. Two distant peaks are volcanic domes. Ute Mountain lies dead ahead, with Antonio Peak standing off to the left, near the Colorado state border. Alluvial sediment, laid down over volcanic ash and lava flows, is traversed by the river through a deep gorge. Its waters are navigable but treacherous at this time of year. Record snowpack in the San Juan Mountains around the headwaters of the

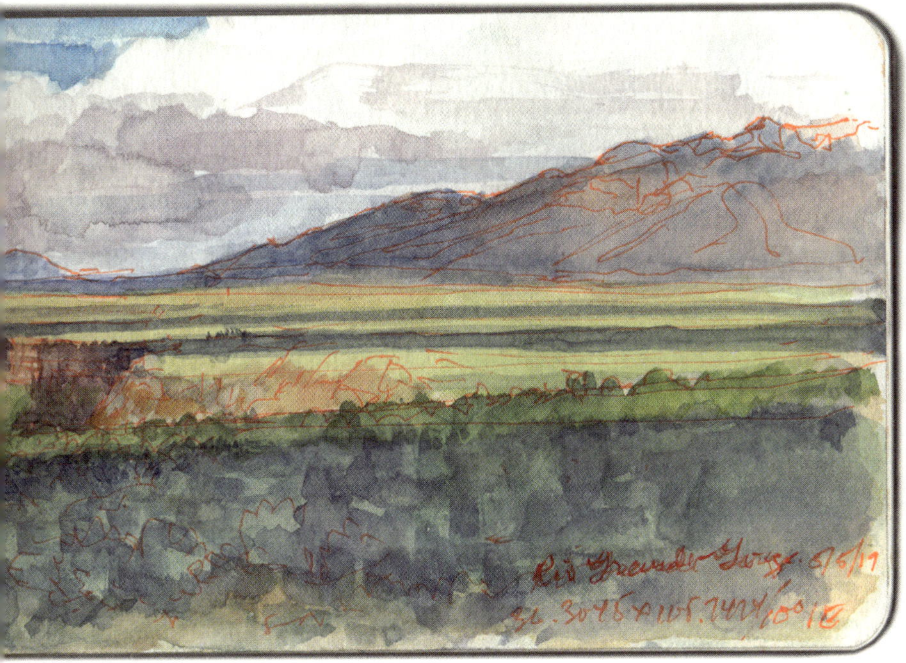

NORTHEAST FROM 36.4105, 105.2424

Rio Grande promised dramatic floodwaters downstream. In such thirsty terrain, the threat of inundation is offset by the benefits of a good drenching. The plateau above the river is watered only by precipitation. The rocky soil is covered in desert sage (*Salvia dorrii*) and piñon pine (*Pinus monophylla*). Taos is at the foot of the mountains to the far right. Across the river, County Road C-8-115 descends to Taos Junction Bridge, just below the confluence of Rio Pueblo de Taos. The road continues south through Orilla Verde and Pilar, terminating at New Mexico Highway 68.

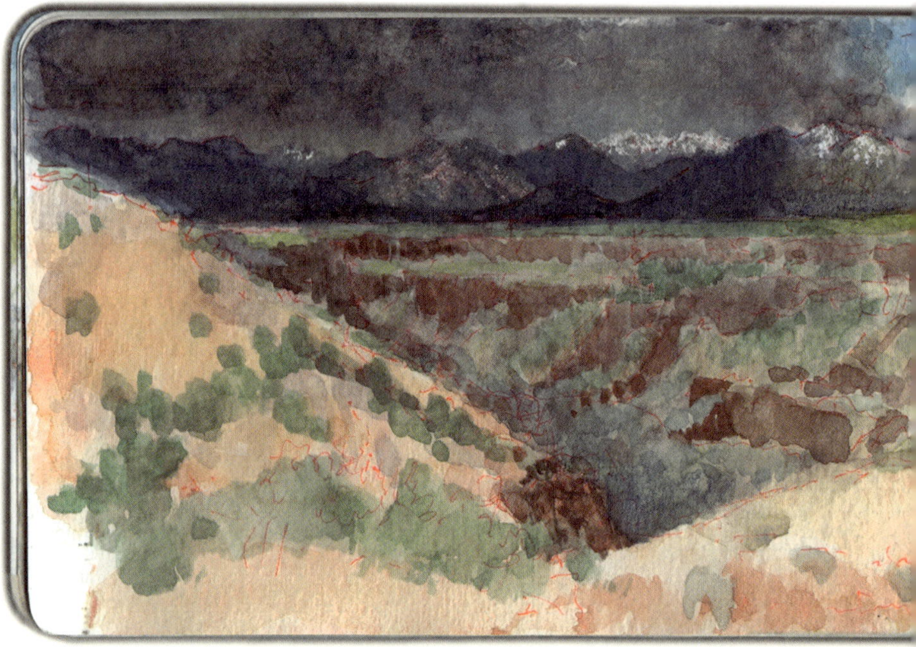

Fig. 7.

FROM THE RIM OF RIO GRANDE GORGE,

Turning to NM567, I guided my car eastward. The road seemed to have been laid down onto the terrain with a straightedge, running from west to east. The land fell away to the south. Red soil gave way to sharp gravel and dark rocks. All was covered by the familiar scattering of sage and piñon, a bushy sea of celadon and jade. Gullies widened into arroyos, revealing rocky layers like icing on a cake, breaking through the soil. Suddenly, the two-lane blacktop made a ninety-degree left-hand turn. Pausing, I looked at the map. State road 567 turned right, winding its way down to Taos Junction Bridge. Descending a gentle grade, I saw the fractured walls of the Rio Grande Gorge come into view. Before the unpaved main road plunged down a rocky series of nerve-wracking switchbacks, I turned left onto the dirt road leading to a

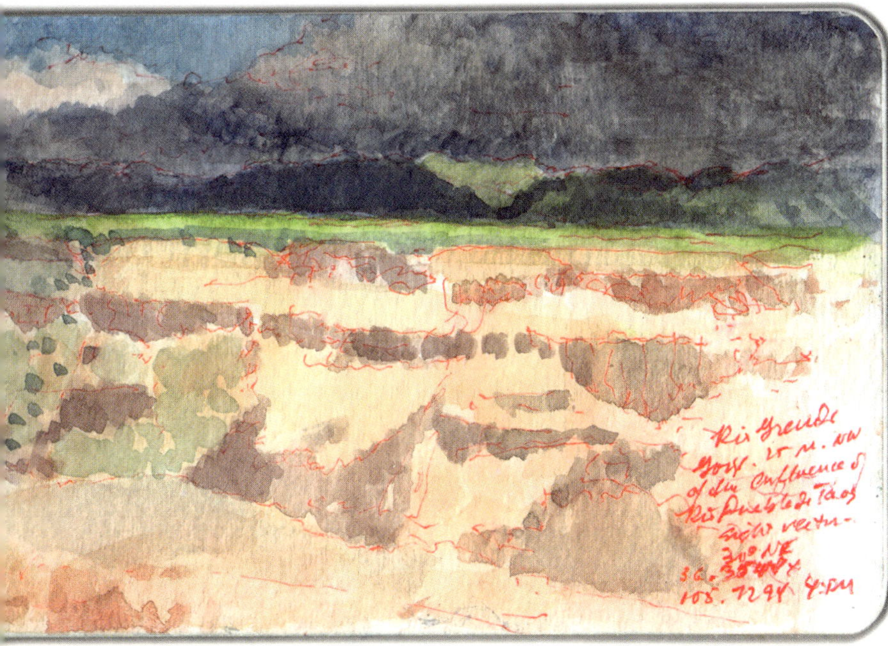

LOOKING NORTHEAST FROM 36.3567, -105.7340

cluster of parked cars. Setting up beside one of the trailheads, I looked to the northeast, opened my sketchbook, gauged depth and distances, and started laying down color. Drawn to the simplicity of the composition, I painted a dark leftward-arrow shape to underscore the distant range of snowcapped mountains. Abstract patterns, rock layers, and vegetation reminded me why this terrain so inspired Marsden Hartley, Georgia O'Keeffe, and others. Thunderclaps crashed behind me. Towering off to the west, black clouds seemed to stride on graphite slabs—diaphanous sheets of driving rain. Peppering the dusty soil, raindrops struck the earth like the .22-caliber bullets that long ago perforated the rusting metal sign in the parking area.

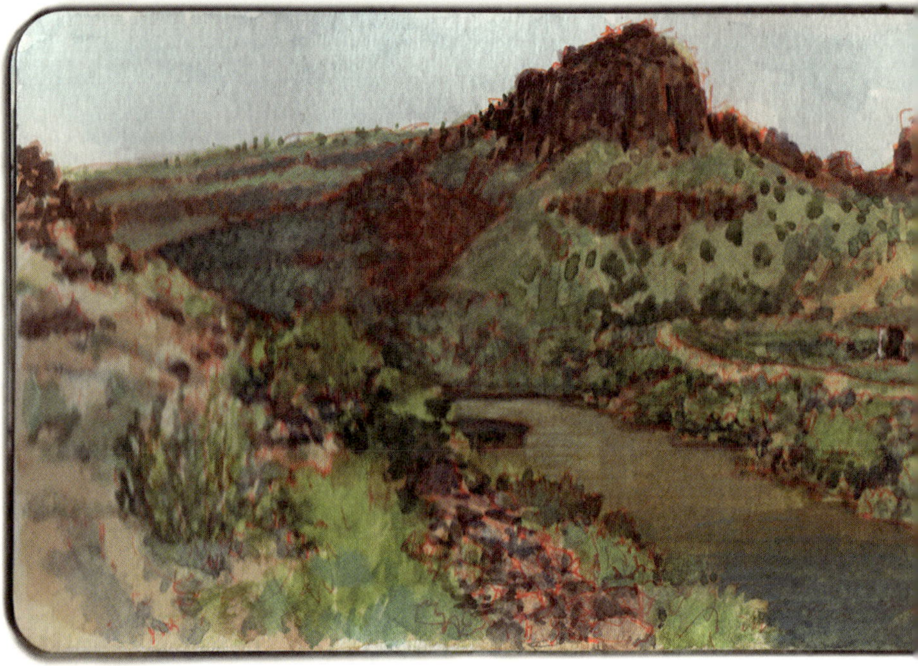

Fig. 8.

CONFLUENCE OF RIO GRANDE DEL NORTE AND RIO PUEBLO

Technically speaking, Taos Junction Bridge is a Pratt-riveted through-truss span located one hundred and fifty yards below the confluence of the Rio Grande del Norte and Rio Pueblo de Taos. The confluence is undramatic, for Rio de Taos joins the great river behind a thick screen of sage and piñon. It might be considered the mouth of the Rio Grande Gorge, even though the river has another twenty-one miles to go before reaching the flood plain at Velarde. On the river's left bank, a dirt road winds its way past campgrounds before ascending to connect with blacktop on the plain above. Below the castle rock, towering above the confluence, is a series of campsites, restrooms, and utility sheds. Below the bridge is a parking area and a boat ramp. Carrying

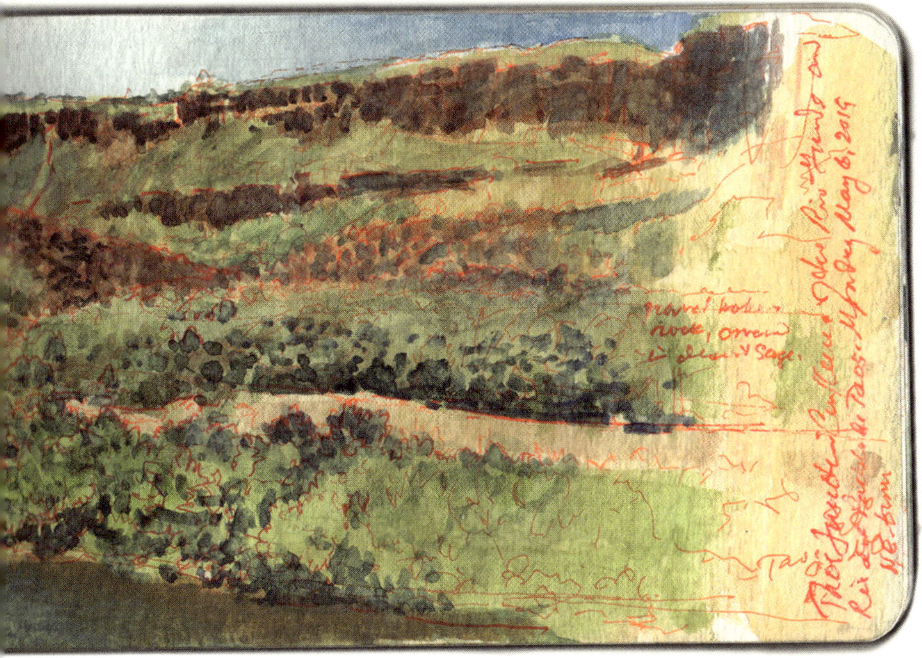

DE TAOS, 59 DEGREES ESE, 36.3354, -105.7346

two kayaks, a car rolled onto the dusty patch of bare soil. Within minutes, paddlers were on the river and away. Passing behind me, two men discussed the stock market as they disappeared into the piñons along the river's edge. A young woman walked onto the bridge to snap a selfie. It was an early May day. Record snowpacks had begun to thaw. Snow melted. The river rose. In a week or two or maybe tomorrow, water might be licking the girders under the bridge. Black clouds rolled in from the west. The mercury dropped. Packing up, I drove back toward Pilar. As I turned south on NM68, the car radio squawked three times, followed by a flash-flood warning.

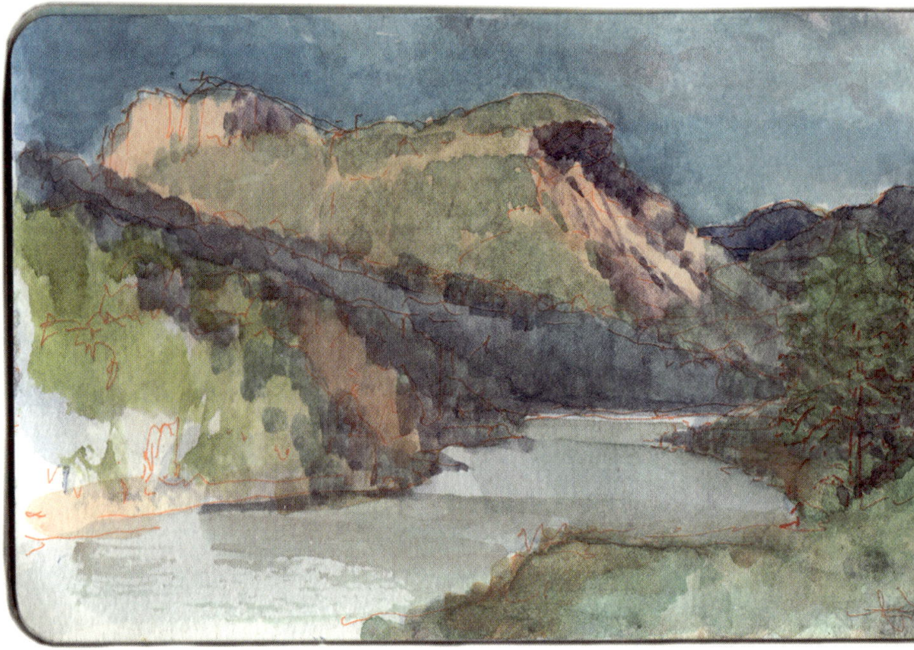

Fig. 9.

ROADSIDE VISTA BELOW PILAR, ROUTE NM68,

Driving north on NM68 past Embudo and a cluster of homes known as Rinconada, motorists are greeted by a distinctive geological formation. A Spanish settlement took root at the base of the hill, on the site of an Apache village destroyed during the reconquest of 1692. In 1795 twenty-five Spanish families took possession of a royal land grant known as Cieneguilla, or "little swamp." The southeastern side of the hill is sheer rock face crowned by a slight overhang. From certain angles, it bears a pareidolic resemblance to devotional images of the Virgin Mary. Seven years after the crucifixion of Christ, the apostle James the Greater preached the Gospel in Iberia. The Blessed Virgin appeared to him on a pillar. Santiago placed the pillar in a

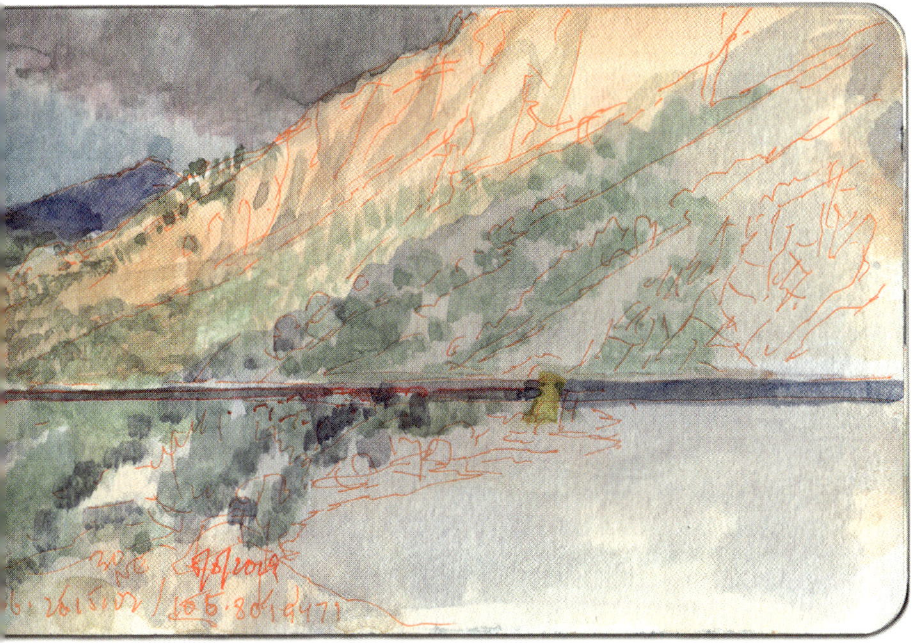

30 DEGREES NE FROM 36.2515102, 105.801947

small church in Zaragoza. The Catedral-Basilica de la Nuestra Señora del Pilar has over the years become one of the holiest sites for Hispanic people. Scraping a living out of the fertile margins of the Rio Grande, Catholic Spaniards must have regarded the hill as a reminder of their protectress. Pilar today is home to the Rio Grande Gorge visitor center, a café, and a rafting tour company. Taos County Road C-115 runs through the village, upriver past Orilla Verde to Taos Junction Bridge. Ascending the crumbling vertiginous walls of the gorge, the unpaved road negotiates a series of hair-raising switchbacks before reaching the wide expanse of the Rio Grande Rift basin.

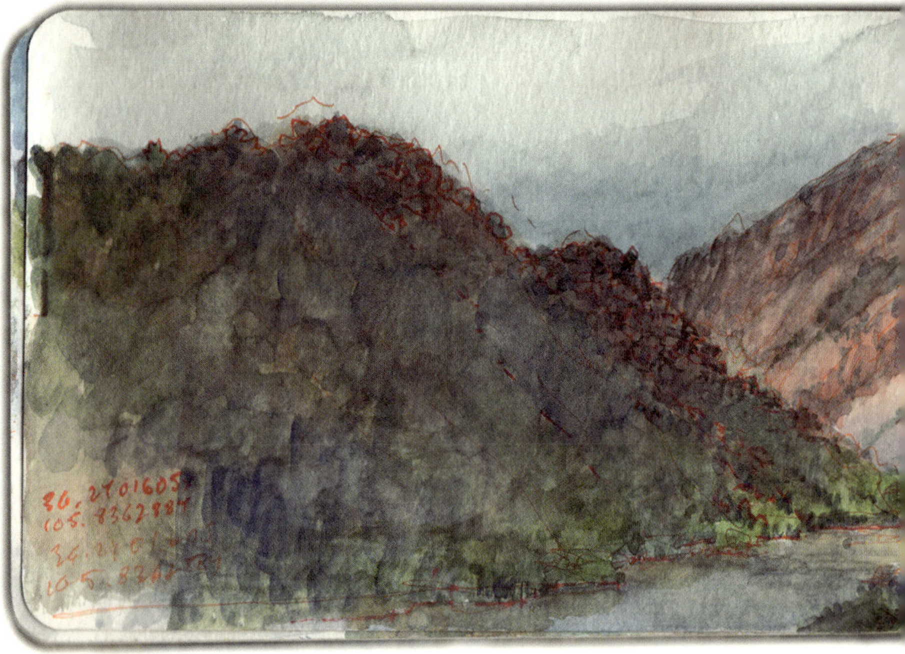

Fig. 10.

BELOW EMBUDO STATION

Heading southwest on NM68, one passes a series of roadside pull-offs frequented by anglers and shutterbugs. On the outbound drive, I had made a note of the steep inclined mountain between Pilar and Embudo, framed between two sloping hills. A few miles downstream is a pair of volcanic plugs, between which Rio Embudo flows through a wooded gap into the Rio Grande. The place-name in Spanish means "bottleneck." Nearby on March 30, 1854, a young bigoted lieutenant rashly led two companies of the US First Regiment of Cavalry into an ambush. Jicarilla Apache and Ute warriors engaged the soldiers in a pitched four-hour battle, forcing the soldiers to withdraw to Rancho de Taos. Considerable losses were suffered on both sides. Native victory was short lived. Eight days later, with Kit Carson serving as guide,

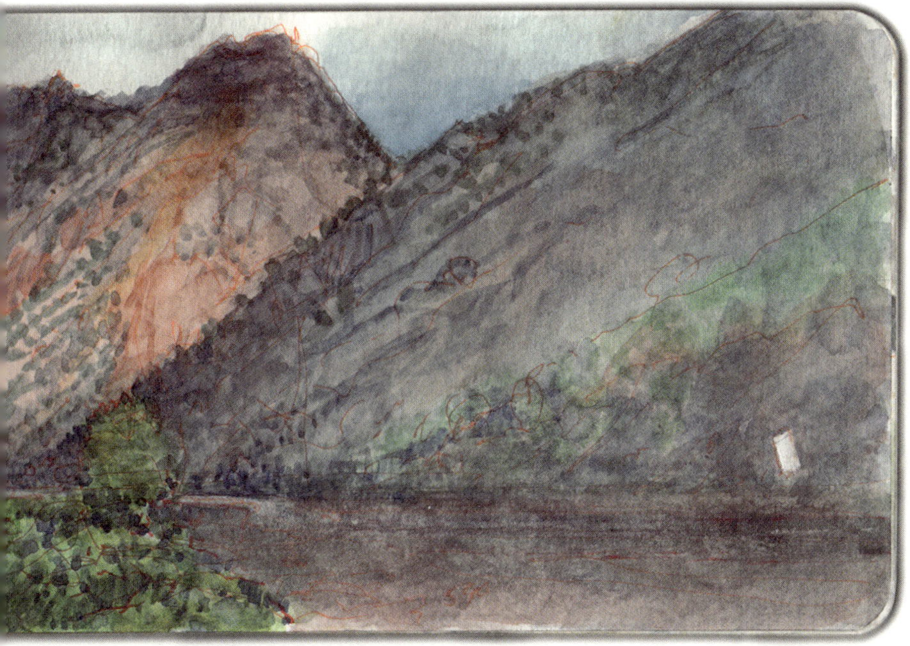

a detachment of the 2nd Calvary Regiment under Lieutenant Philip St. George Cooke fell upon the war party at Ojo Caliente. Many who survived the attack perished from exposure. In a note of irony, Carson had been on a mission to offer the Native combatants rations and humanitarian aid as the battle raged. The present-day village was established in 1881 as a watering station for the Chili Line of the Denver and Rio Grande Western Railroad. Seven years later the hamlet was selected by the explorer John Wesley Powell as a stream-gauging station for the United States Geological Survey. The Embudo Historic District was added to the National Register of Historic Places in 1979—coincidentally the year of my first visit to New Mexico.

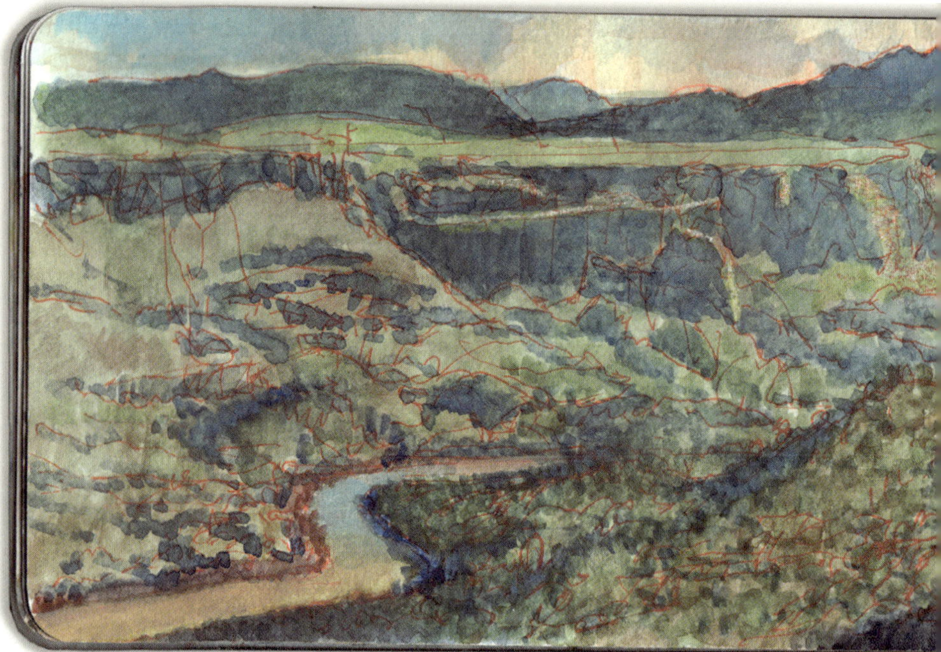

Fig. 11.

WHITE ROCK CANYON, LATE LIGHT

People often visited me while I worked. One day, I was painting on a rocky outcropping half a mile south of the point. An Anglo couple approached. The man calmly told me that when he was a boy, he and a friend used to comb the canyon for artifacts, looting graves when they found them. His friend still has a couple of skulls on his dresser at home. The man confessed that it troubled him; it didn't seem right. I suggested that it would be best to return whatever things he had removed. No good can ever come from tampering with the dead. If he was interested in the Indigenous culture, he should read about it or talk to the people. Understanding their ways might

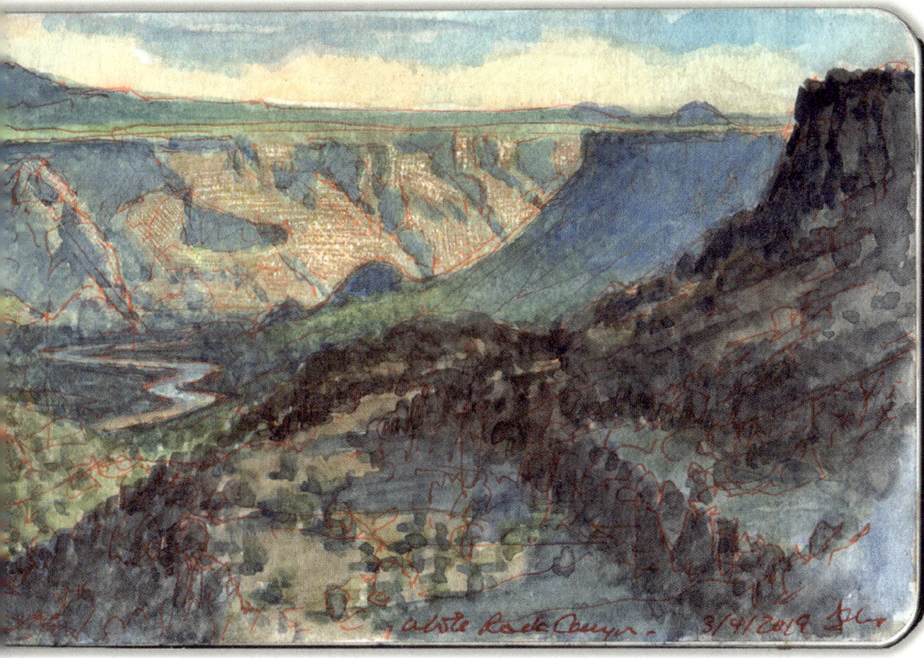

inspire greater respect. While some Puebloans may earn a living from fry-bread tourism and art sales, any diffidence toward non-Natives is well founded. As on many of my forays, I had begun multiple compositions of different views from the western rim of the canyon. Warm sunlight and cool shadows carved marvelous forms in its eastern walls. A large hawk glided past, following the canyon rim. Landing in the piñon tree beside me, a crow greeted me with a squawk. My keys lay atop my field bag. I put them in my pocket.

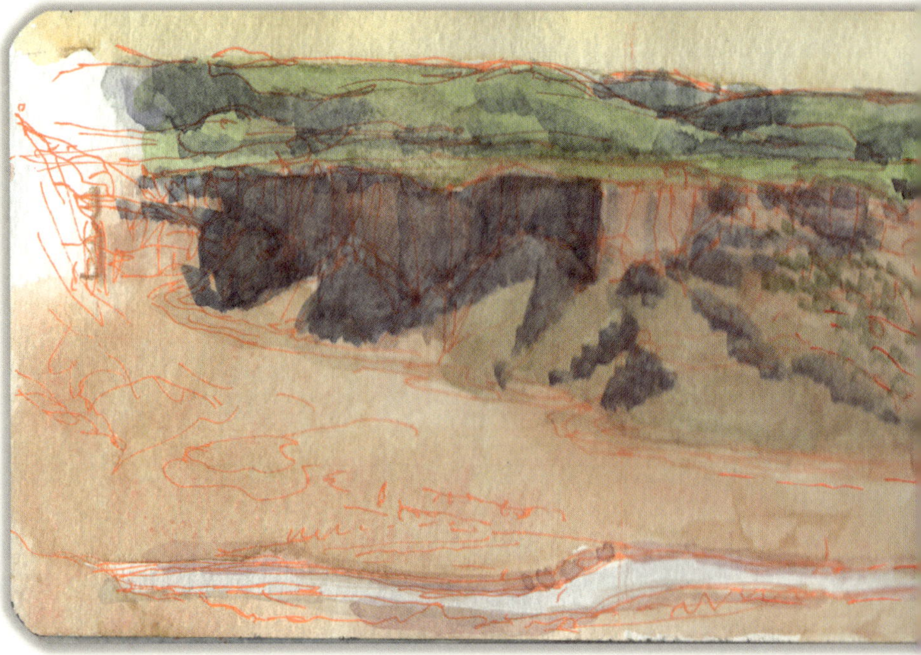

Fig. 12.

WHITE ROCK CANYON, SOUTH-SOUTHEAST FROM

Two of my painting locations between the headwaters of the Rio Grande and the Albuquerque Basin resonate deeply with me. Embarking on the production of a series of monotypes with the Santa Fe master printer Mike Costello, I chose as the subjects of the prints the confluence of the Rio Grande with Rio Pueblo de Taos and White Rock Canyon. I suppose there was a narrative appeal, since both represent key points on the downstream course of the river. Both are magnets for outdoor recreation. Both possess visual features that are at once iconic and specific. Taos Junction Bridge, within the Orilla Verde Recreation Area, is not to be confused with Taos Junction twenty-five miles to the west. Rising above the confluence like the prow of a ship is a rocky butte where the desert floor tapers to a high point

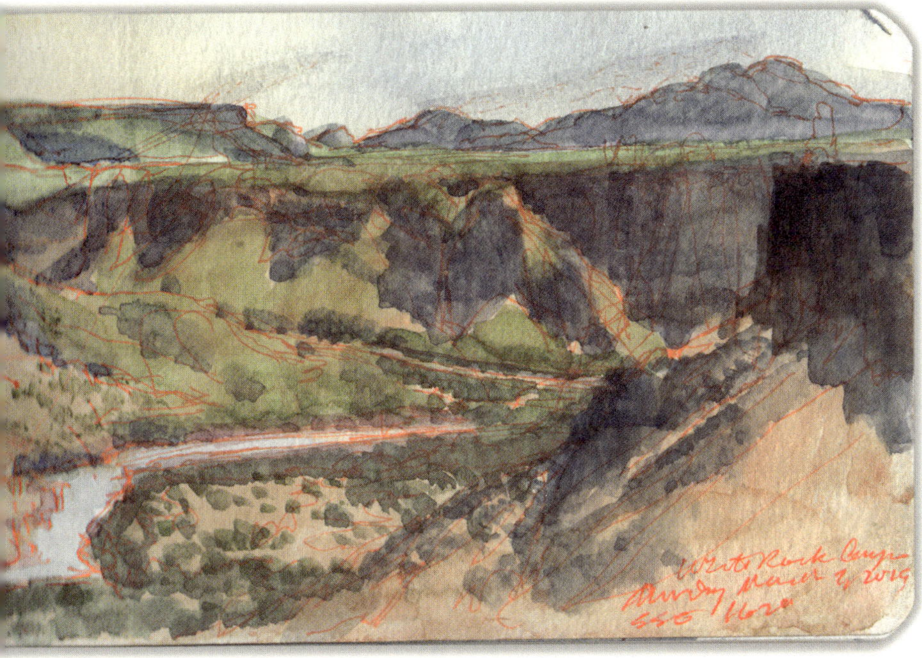

36.8257, -106.1809

of land between the two rivers. Like Moran's Green River Cliffs or Cézanne's Mont Sainte-Victoire, it meets all the criteria of a painter's motif. From the canyon rim, the serpentine river runs a muddy course between sandy banks and an avalanche of basalt—sharp rocks shorn from the vertiginous Pajarito escarpment. Setting to work, I made a checklist of precedents: Moran's Yellowstone, Turner's Reichenbach Falls, Corot's Pont de Narni—elevated perspectives that assume a magisterial gaze. Smithson's *Spiral Jetty*, Christo and Jeanne-Claude's *Valley Curtain*, and the panoramas of Rackstraw Downes crowded my mind. The challenge facing me was to forget them all for a moment, to see without prejudice all that I found before me.

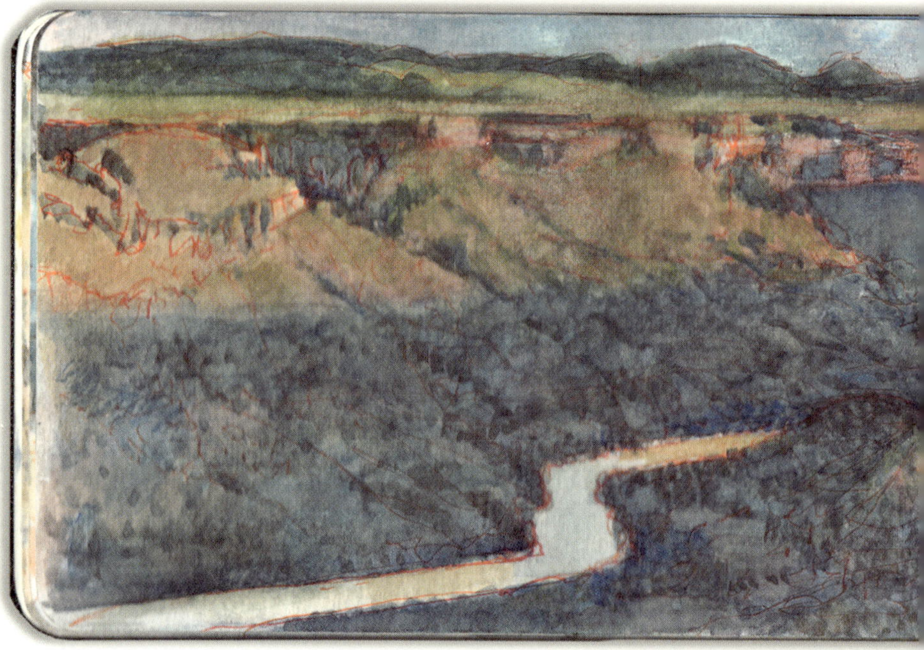

Fig. 13.

WHITE ROCK CANYON, SUNSET

White Rock Canyon is a stunning declivity carved by the Rio Grande through volcanic sediment, running south from Otowi Peak, aka Buckman Mesa. Winding through the bottom of White Rock Canyon, the Rio Grande runs narrow and swift on its way to Cochiti Reservoir. Resembling the geology of the much deeper gorge forty miles to the north, basaltic uplifts towering above heaps of rock fall ascend from ribbons of greenery along the river-banks. An old spur of the narrow-gauge Denver & Rio Grande Railroad known as the Chili Line stopped at Diablo Canyon, at the confluence of Cañada Ancha, a seasonal creek bed across the Rio Grande from White Rock. Steam locomotives were no less thirsty than living things in such a parched land, and thus like El Camino Real de Tierra Adentro, the railroad followed the

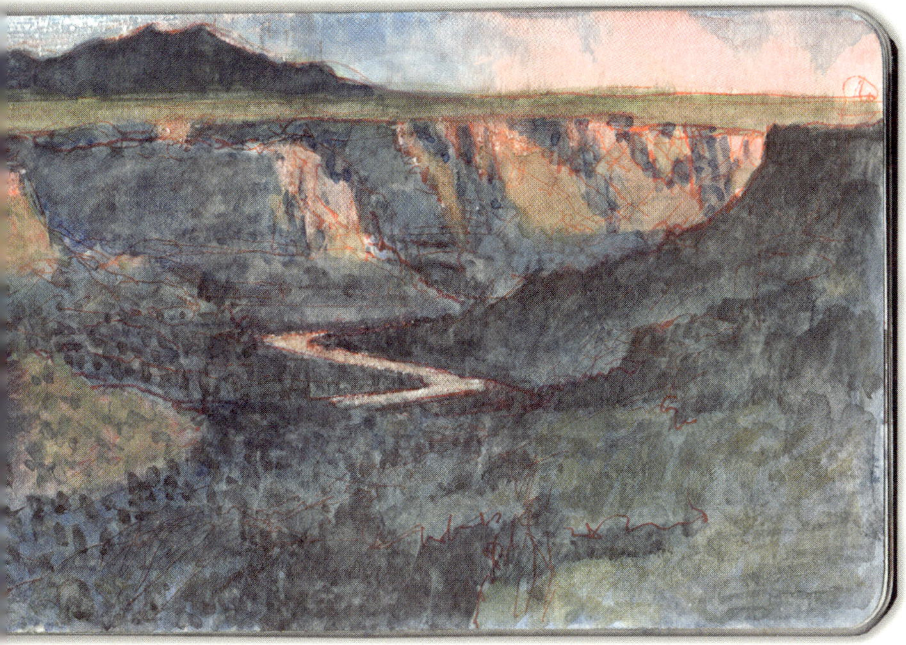

river. The decision to build a narrow-gauge railroad (less than the standard gauge of 56.5 inches) may have been predicated on access to water as much as by challenging terrain. In the 1960s temporary housing built for employees at Los Alamos Nuclear Laboratory along the western rim of the canyon was replaced by permanent homes, schools, shopping, parks, playing fields, and hiking trails. Signs caution hikers to be on the lookout for rattlesnakes, which tend to concentrate in areas that allow them to find subterranean dens suitable for winter hibernation. At 6,500 feet of altitude, White Rock Canyon approaches the uppermost extremity of their range. I was optimistic that the first week of March was too early for these predators to be too obstreperous.

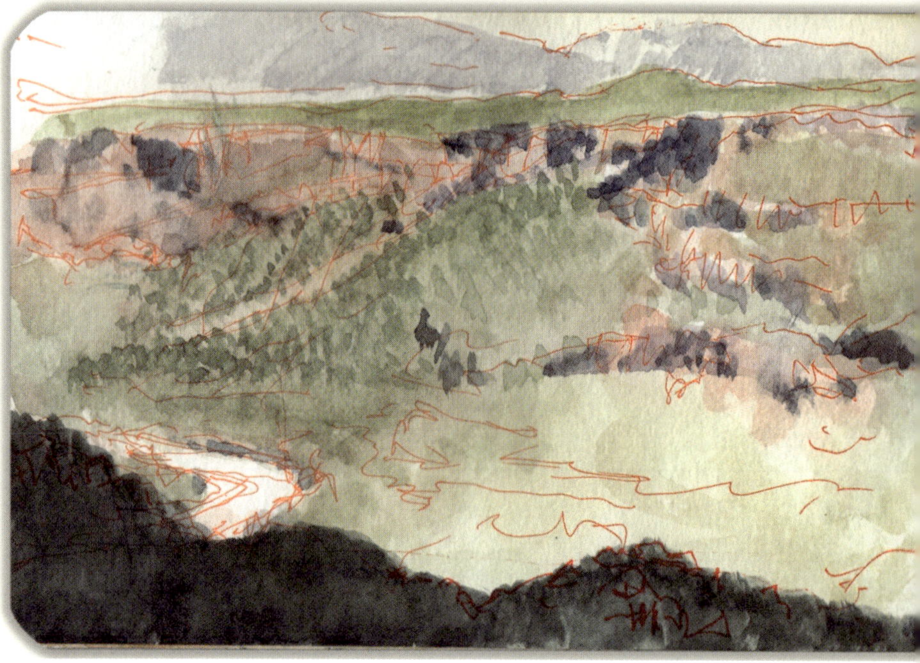

Fig. 14.

WHITE ROCK CANYON, EAST-NORTHEAST FROM

Formed by the combined effect of alluvial sedimentation with volcanic activity, the Pajarito Plateau stretches from Valles Caldera in the Jemez Mountains in the west to the Sangre de Cristo range in the east. Marking its northernmost boundary is a concatenation of mesas running alongside a dry creek that meets the right bank of the Rio Grande near Otowi Bridge, then east from Buckman Mesa toward Pojoaque. Forming the northern bluffs above Cochiti Reservoir, the southern escarpment of the plateau is known as Cerro La Bajada farther east, where the land drops precipitously to the south into the Albuquerque Basin. Named for nearby tuff and pumice deposits, White Rock Canyon is actually a series of canyons carved through multiple strata of volcanic ash and Bandelier Tuff deposited by the eruption

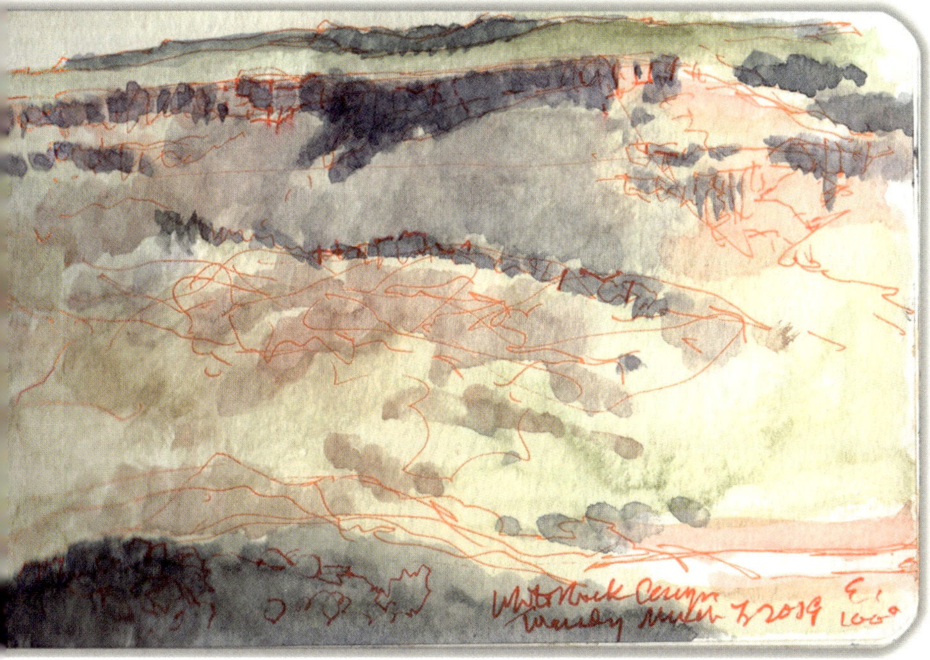

36.8257, -106.1809

of the Valles super-volcano to the west, together with basalt deposits generated by the Cerro de Rio volcanic field east of the canyon. Like the Rio Grande Gorge and the Wild Rivers Recreation Area farther upstream, parts of the canyon appear to be a layer cake of sheer drops and disorderly heaps of rock fall. The canyon's eastern wall exhibits fewer cliff faces. Vertical basalt formations emerge as sharp ribbons of dark rock, pushing out from under the promiscuous landslide. Under a blazing sunlight during the early afternoon, these features dissolve into abstract patterns of pale hues. The western rim where I stood seemed by contrast to be cast into an umbrageous gloom, as the distant mountains glowed a faraway blue.

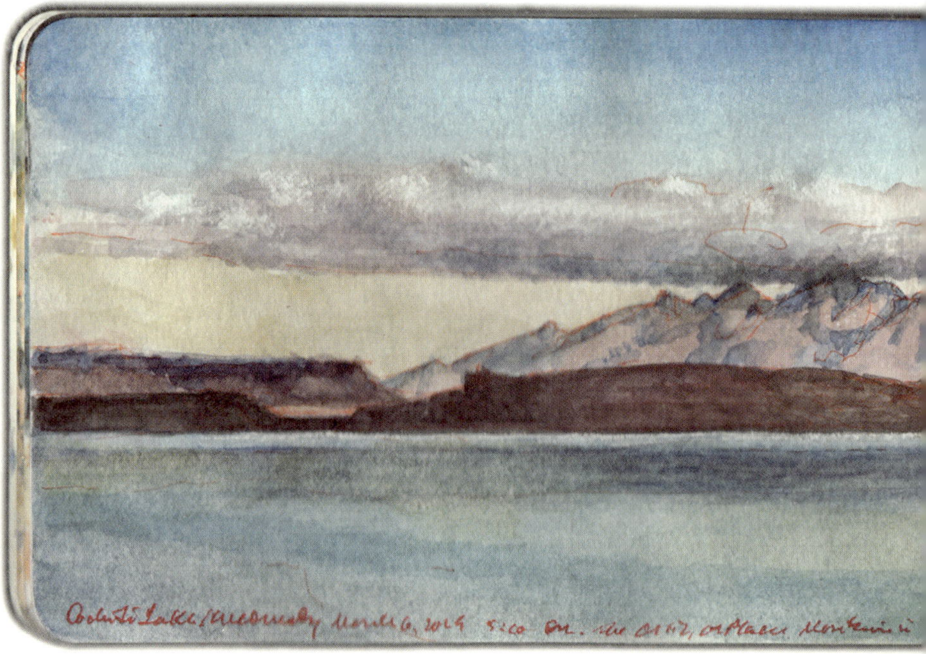

Fig. 15.

COCHITI LAKE AND DAM, SOUTHEAST FROM

When I first visited Cochiti Pueblo in 1980, the reservation was open to public use. Unpaved roads led north to the ash fields and cañadas below Valles Caldera or west to the tent rocks at Kasha-Katuwe, Keresan for "white hills" In 2001 the area was designated a national monument. Populations in Santa Fe and Albuquerque have doubled over the past thirty years, which led Cochiti to close its lands to the uninvited. Today, visitors are greeted by a modern welcome center, café, and gift shop. One of the few areas open to the public is Cochiti Dam. Driving toward the hamlet of Cochiti Lake, I turned right, passing a cluster of tribal utility buildings. Veering right again, the road descended a long incline that terminated at a boat landing with a

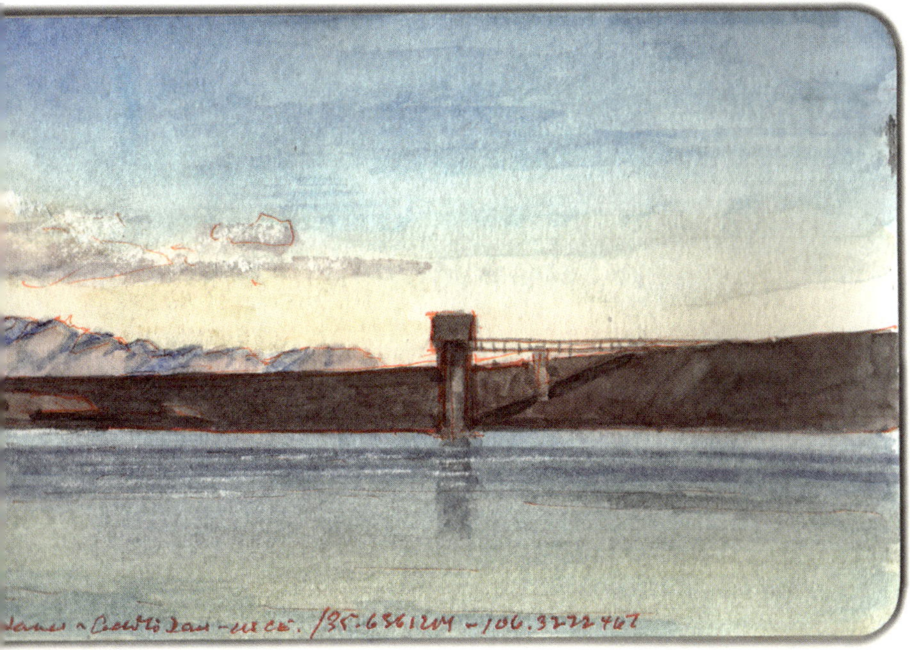

35.6361204, 106.333467

short dock to its left. A local man stood in the water, wrestling his boat onto a trailer. Flanking the boat ramp were short stretches of beach. Carrying my gear across the boat ramp, I sat down at one of the concrete picnic tables behind the beach. I was the only non-Indigenous person onsite. A young couple sat at the next table, staring into their cellphones. A fisherman walked by, looked at me, and nodded. One must expect a degree of diffidence from Native Americans toward Anglos visiting Indian land. I was also mindful that the lake and its shores are under the control of the Army Corps of Engineers, which adds yet another level of stress to the delicate ethnic symbiosis in the Land of Enchantment.

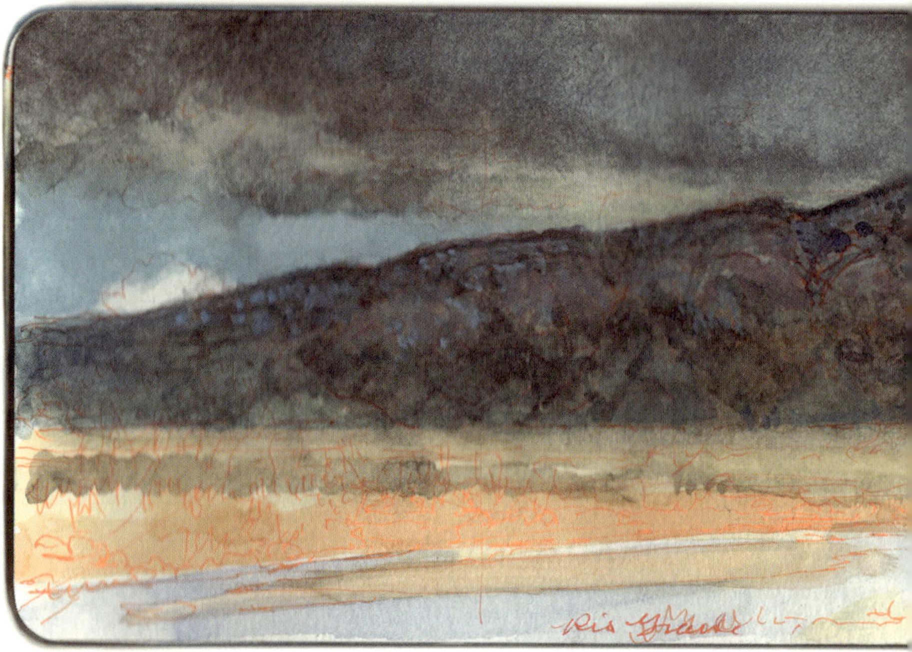

Fig. 16.

SANDIA MOUNTAINS FROM KUAUA

Rising four thousand feet above the Albuquerque basin of the Rio Grande Rift, the summit of Sandia Peak is nearly eleven thousand feet. A fault-block uplift consisting of granite capped with a three-hundred-foot layer of fossil-rich Pennsylvania limestone, it has a steep western face. The eastern slope is gradual. Its arcing crest and pinkish color in fading sunlight resembled a watermelon to famished Spaniards, who dubbed the mountains "Sandia." Puebloans called it Posu gai hoo-oo, "where water slides down." The Rio Grande flows southward past the western foot of this formation. Twelve thousand years of human habitation are evidenced by Paleo-Indian sites in, around, and beneath the meandering river. New agrarian communities sprang up along its banks following the collapse of Chacoan culture

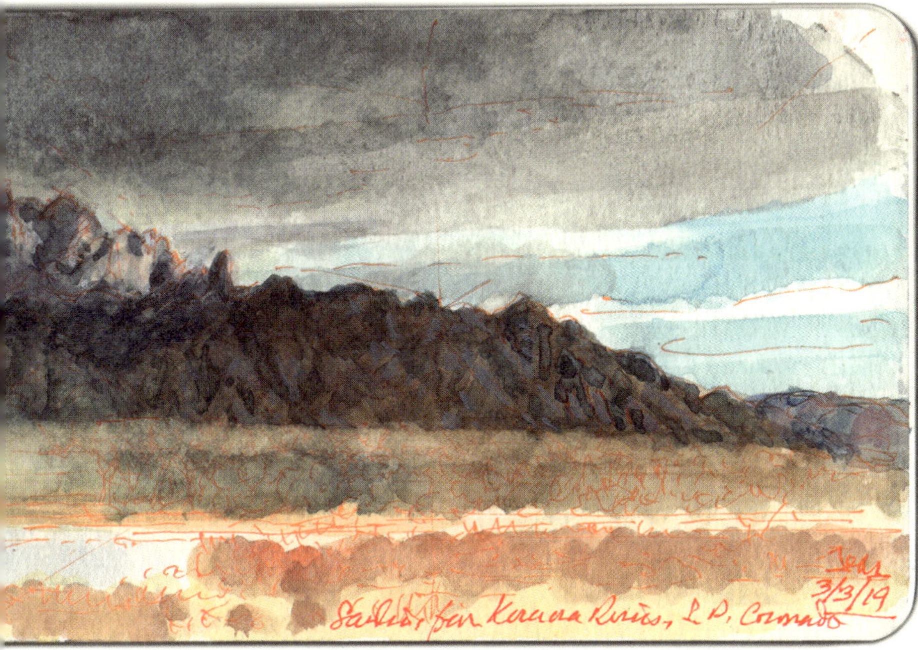

beginning in the twelfth century. In 1540 in the vicinity of present-day Bernalillo and Albuquerque, the conquistador Francisco Vázquez de Coronado y Luján and his army enjoyed the hospitality of the Tiguex pueblos that they did not first destroy. The sudden arrival of an additional two thousand mouths to feed strained the modest resources of these Indigenous farming communities. Back from his failed attempt to locate golden Quivira on the high plains of Kansas, Coronado again occupied Kuaua the following winter. Recuperating from injuries sustained while falling from his horse, Coronado decided to return to Mexico, leaving behind a few friars to teach the Gospel. Kuaua was abandoned sometime about 1600. The partially reconstructed pueblo is now open to visitors as a state park.

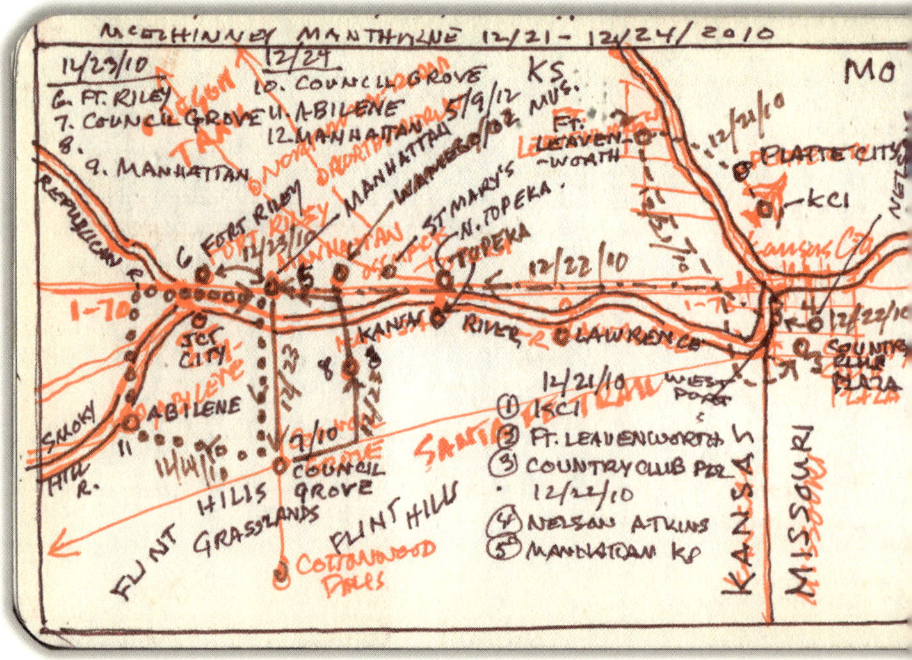

Fig. 17.

MAP OF ROAD TRIP FROM KANSAS CITY TO

Drawn to maps from an early age, I am fascinated by ancient cartography. Framed with scenes of faraway places, old maps might feature Natives in colorful dress and sea monsters licking their margins. Delineated in hachures, strata of elevation were rendered in radiating pen strokes. Hills and mountains seem to jump off the page, like the vacuum-formed plastic relief maps that once adorned schoolroom walls. Mapping and surveying are fundamental to expeditionary practice. In journal painting, I will sometimes use the book gutter as my line of sight, recording the compass heading in the margins of the drawing. On road trips following tight schedules, there is no time to stop and sketch. Sitting in a motel at day's end, I might produce a map to record my progress. This practice began years ago with marking up road maps

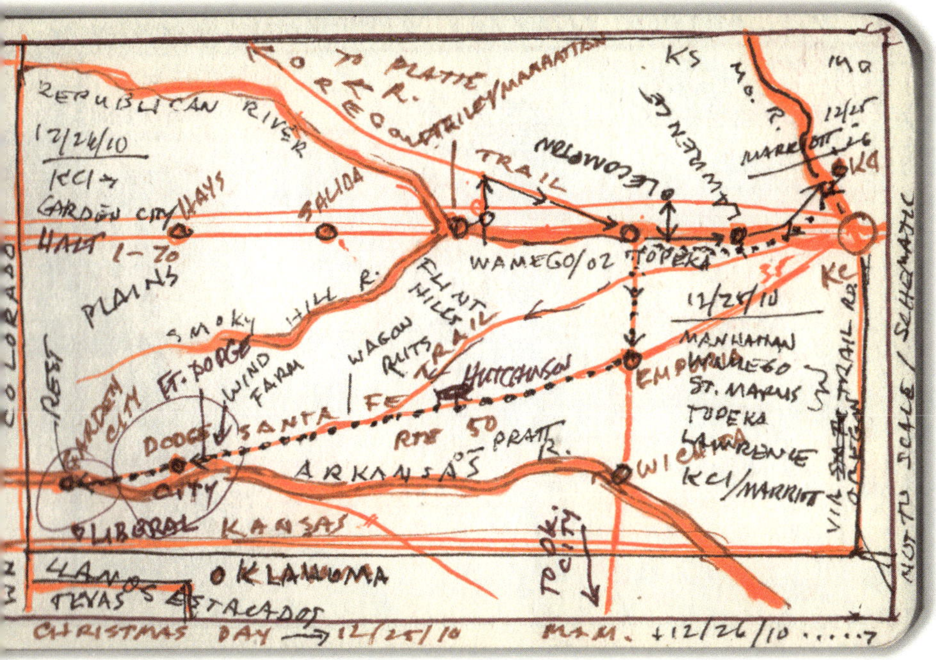

MONUMENT VALLEY, DECEMBER 25–29, 2010

purchased at service stations or picked up at welcome centers. Fluorescent markers highlighted my routes. Incidents of travel were recorded in scrawling marginalia. During lunch at a diner on Route 66, the placemat caught my eye. Crawling from corner to corner across the scalloped sheet, the legendary highway was dotted with stopping points, flanked by texts and vignettes of scenic attractions. Besmirched with coffee stains and biscuit gravy, my placemat was a goner. The waitress brought me a fresh one. Pushing my dishes aside, I made a few notes. Unfolding it later that night, I transferred lunchtime scribbles into my sketchbook. Almost by chance my practice had grown, inspired by a placemat.

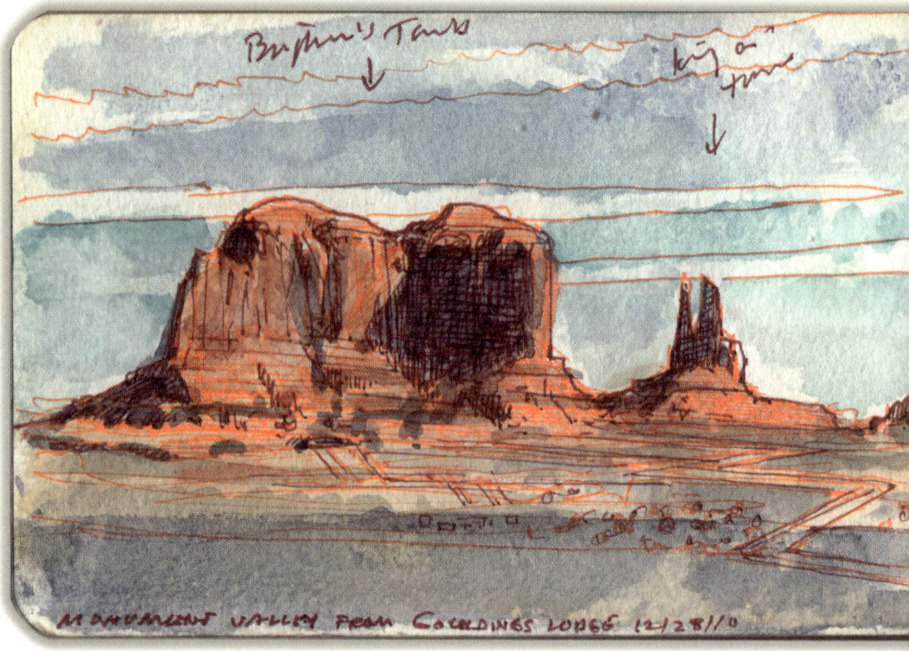

Fig. 18.

FOUR BUTTES FROM GOULDING'S LODGE, TSÉ BII

Saturday, December 25, 2010. Walking up to the car rental desk at Kansas City airport, I laid the contract on the counter. The attendant asked for our flight number. Looking it up, he calmly informed us that due to a blizzard on the East Coast, nothing was flying in or out of any New York City airport. I asked if he could find out how long it would continue. Placing another call, he informed us that it would be five or six days before we could get seats on another flight. No guarantee, but maybe next Thursday or Friday. He also informed us that a massive winter storm was brewing on the Pacific coast. Snow had fallen in Los Angeles for the first time in many years. My wife, Kathie, looked at me and asked, "How far is it from here to Monument

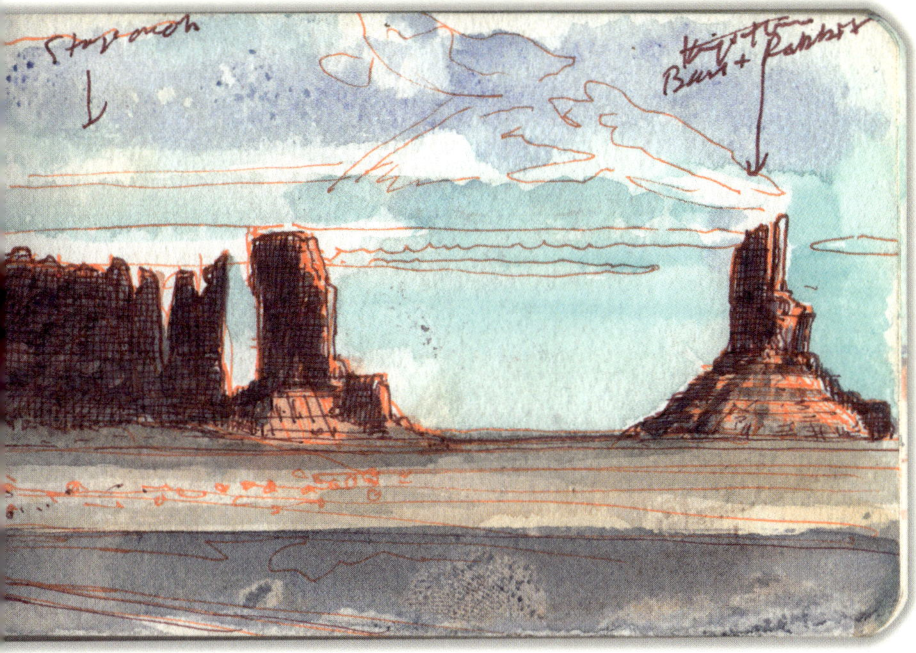

NDZISGAII (MONUMENT VALLEY, NAVAJO NATION)

Valley?" Trying to compose a quick, coherent answer, I calculated the distance, potential delays, and challenges of getting back in time to catch our return flight, then gave her my answer: "Let's go." Three days later we arrived at Goulding's Lodge, the guest ranch and hotel used by John Ford as a base camp when filming many of his westerns. Famous for its spectacular chessboard of tall sandstone buttes, it became synonymous with the cinematic West. Needless to say, the Diné have other names for these formations. I drew this sketch upon our arrival: from left to right, Brigham's Tomb, King-in-His-Throne, Stagecoach, and Bear-and-Rabbit.

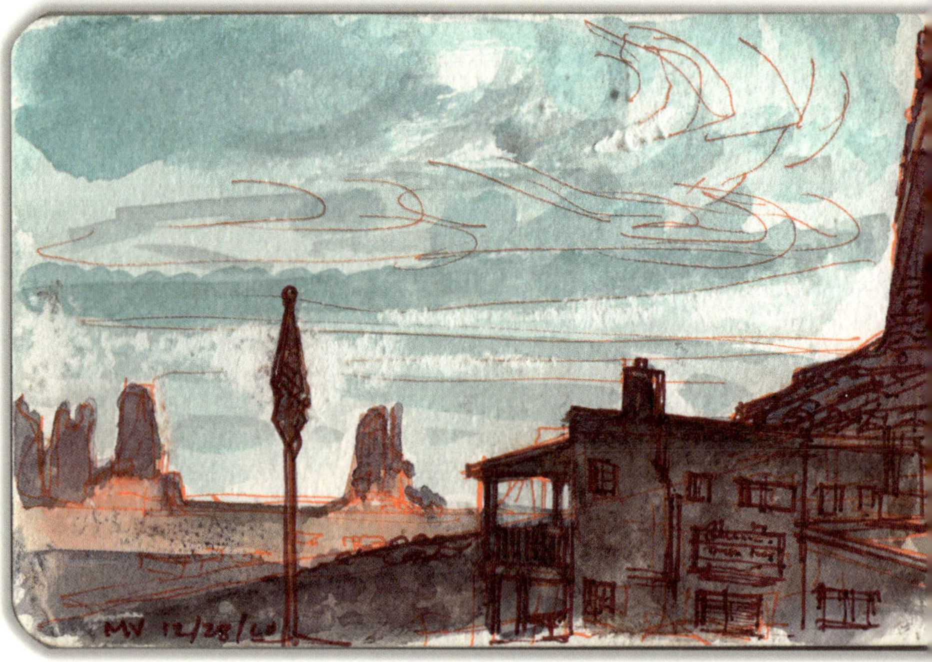

Fig. 19.

MONUMENT VALLEY FROM GOULDING'S LODGE

In 1928 the Colorado native and World War I veteran Harry Goulding purchased six hundred acres from the Navajo Nation at Paiute Strip, nor far from a restaurant owned by his cousin. Raising sheep and operating a trading post, Goulding had a few Hollywood connections through in-laws who worked in the film industry. Hearing that the John Ford was looking for a location to shoot his new film, *Stagecoach*, Goulding sent photographs of Monument Valley to the director. The stunning scenery appealed to Ford's vision of the West, with the added bonus that it was too far from Tinseltown for studio executives to just drop in during a shoot. Over the years, Goulding expanded the property, building guest cottages and later a hotel and gift shop. Ford's movies put Monument Valley on the map, generating tourism revenue for

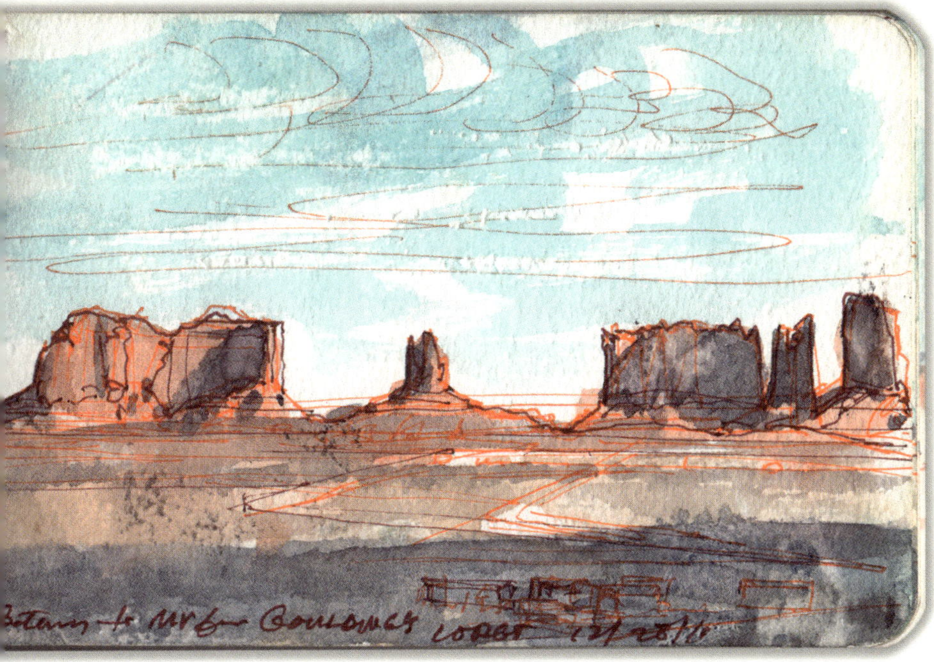

the Gouldings and the Navajo community. My only prior view of Monument Valley was through field glasses twenty years earlier, viewed from the high road between Chinle and Canyon de Chelly. Having caught glimpses of Goulding's Lodge in newsreels and documentaries, I was surprised to find the modest complex at the foot of a high sandstone cliff. Parked beside it was a stagecoach. The old trading post had become a museum. Named after film stars, all the original guest cabins were occupied. We grabbed the last available room, located at the farthest end of a newish low-rise motel building. Waiting in the restaurant for our guide to arrive, I produced this sketch. We ordered a Navajo taco and could finish only half.

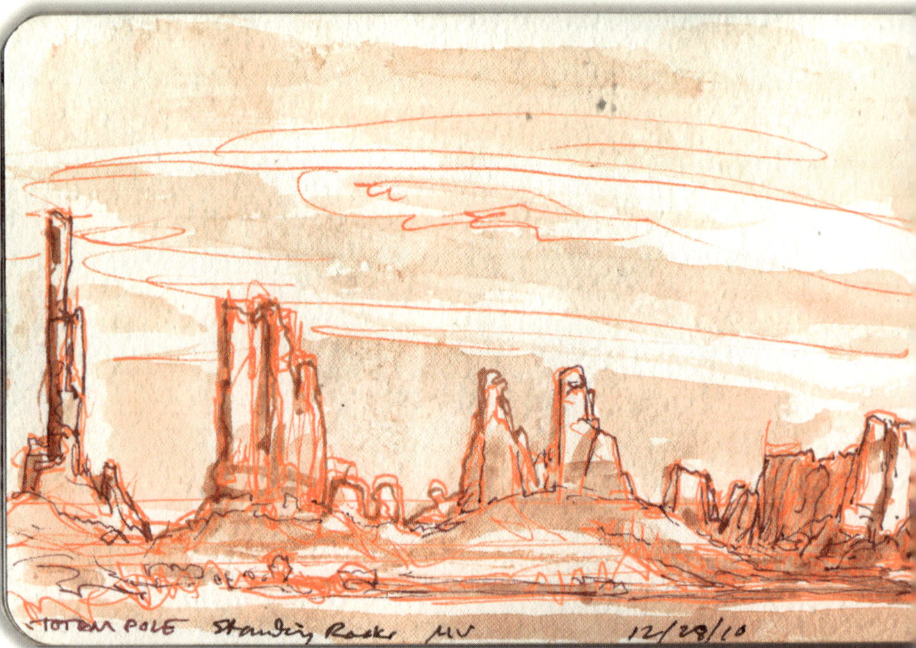

Fig. 20.

MONOCHROMATIC STUDY, MONUMENT VALLEY

The westerns that John Ford filmed in black and white never suffered from a lack of color. Although color film stock and processing were more expensive, by the 1930s shooting in black and white had come to be recognized as an aesthetic decision as much as a matter of cost. Technicolor might work for epics and fantasies for audiences clamoring for eye candy, but it was not always appropriate for serious drama, suspense, or westerns. Forcing filmgoers to imagine colors helped audiences suspend their belief in other ways. In expeditionary art, color was often regarded as embellishment—nonessential data reserved for deluxe editions and prints suitable for framing. In a practical sense, the function of chorographic drawing was to provide a

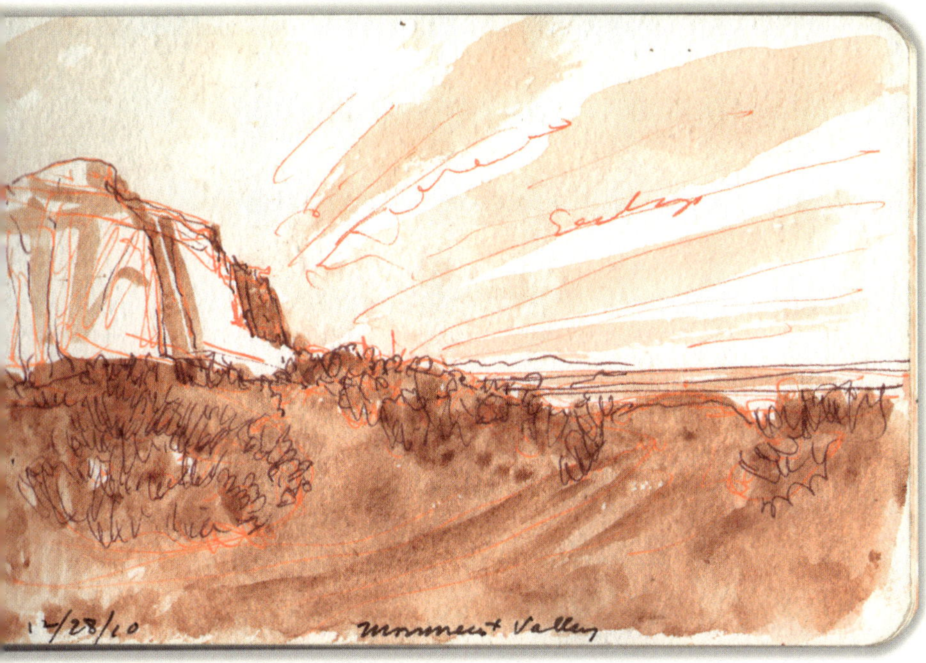

view from the ground of what a map would describe from an aerial perspective. As with drawing the human figure, there are steps to be followed, from movement and proportion to bone, muscle, and flesh. In black-and-white prints, color could be indicated by a secret code of line patterns that told the hand-colorist which hues to apply and where. In quick field sketches, many artists simply write on their work, indicating blue here, ocher there, and so forth. I drew this sketch during a ten-minute stop from the back seat of a four-wheel-drive Jeep being driven by our Navajo guide. It is noteworthy that this Standing Up Country somehow eluded early explorers, who managed to visit Canyon de Chelly and other nearby sites.

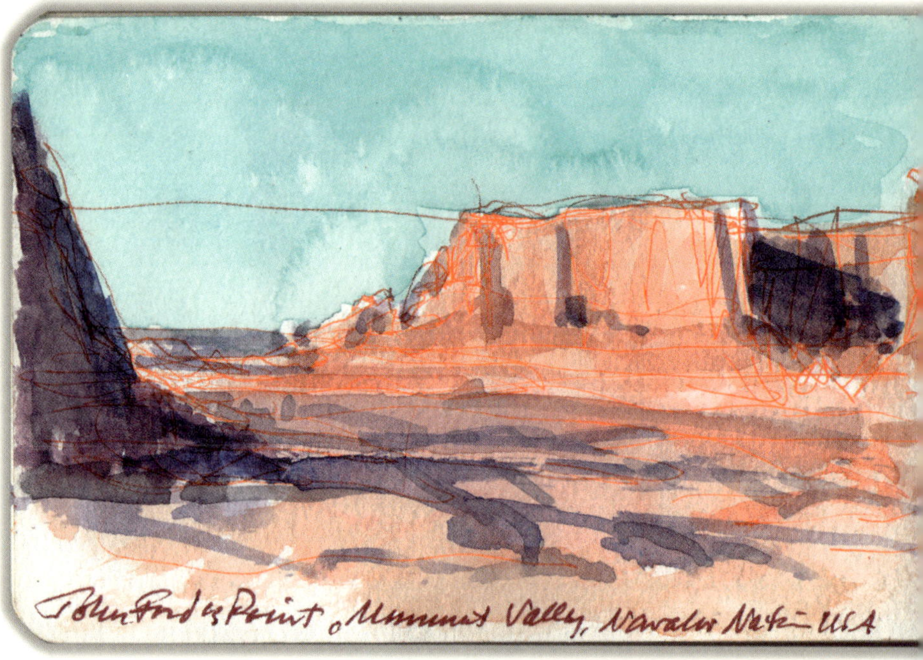

Fig. 21.

JOHN FORD'S POINT, MONUMENT VALLEY,

Checking into Goulding's Lodge on a late December day, my wife and I dumped our bags. Our room was located at the far end of a modern addition on the same level as the restaurant. The celebrity rooms had all been taken, as had most of the accommodations at the View, a newly built resort and hotel inside the tribal park. We hired a local guide—a diffident fellow, mid-sixties, wearing weathered denim and a fur-felt cowboy hat. Being driven in a high-clearance white Jeep with giant tires and roll bar, we passed the View. Our guide explained that a couple of Anglos raised the capital. Married to local girls, they got a pass on tribal zoning restrictions. I never fact-checked his story. It was a reminder that although tourism dollars were

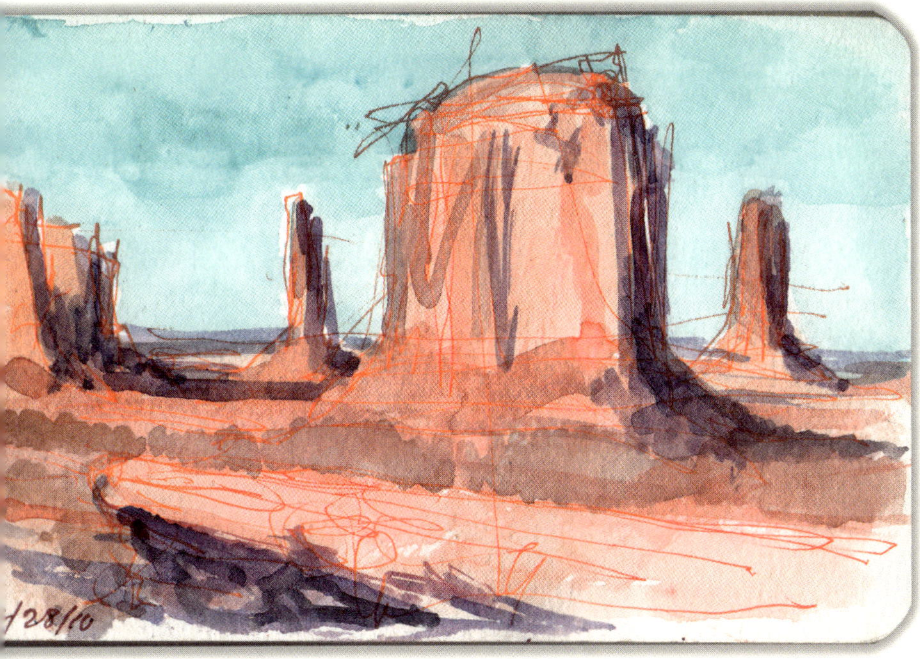

DECEMBER 28, 2010

welcome, outsiders were another matter. A popular destination within the park is a narrow rocky outcropping known as John Ford Point, named for the director of *Stagecoach*, *The Searchers*, and other classic westerns. Visitors park in a pull-off, then walk down a short trail. Reaching the feature, one runs a gauntlet of local artisans peddling Native jewelry and other keepsakes. For a fee you can get on a horse, which is walked onto the rocky diving board. Pictures are taken, just as in the movies. I shot a photo of Kathie, *sin caballo*. Amid the ruckus, I produced a hasty sketch, later elaborating it back in our hotel room. Before dawn I discovered our car covered in snow, which continued to fall.

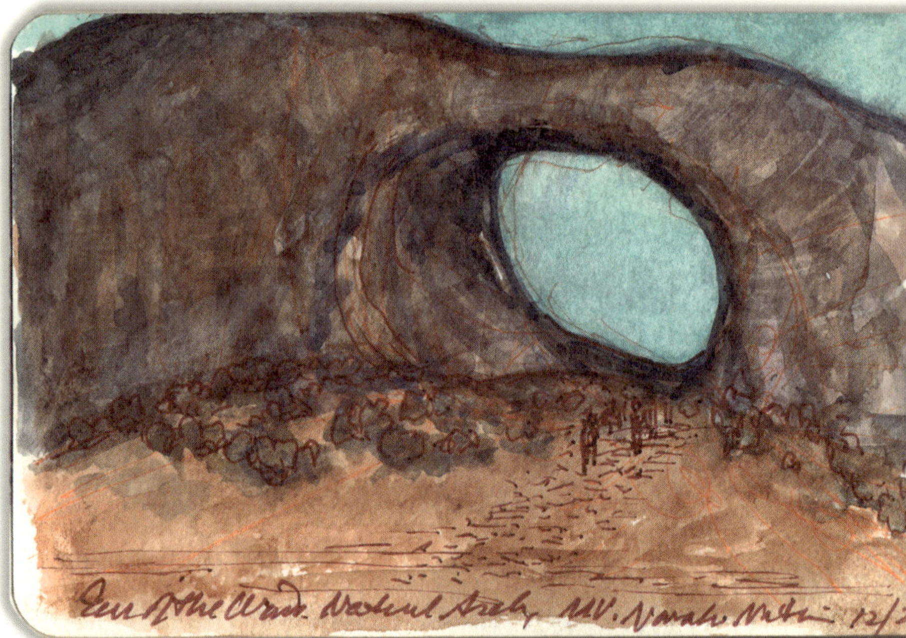

Fig. 22.

EAR OF THE WIND, MONUMENT VALLEY

Like many geological features within Monument Valley Tribal Park, Ear of the Wind seems to have been concocted by the same kind of marketing magic that transformed Marion Morrison into John Wayne. The circular aperture in a large outcropping of de Chelly sandstone was formed by the process of chemical exfoliation. Entering the rock, water dissolves the small particles that act as a binder. Loosening larger grains in the sandstone accelerates the natural process of erosion. Moisture gathers in rocky niches, which are enlarged by persistent winds that carry away the exfoliated particles. In igneous dikes and other geological formations with high aspect ratios, openings can appear that become stone arches over time. Ear of the Wind

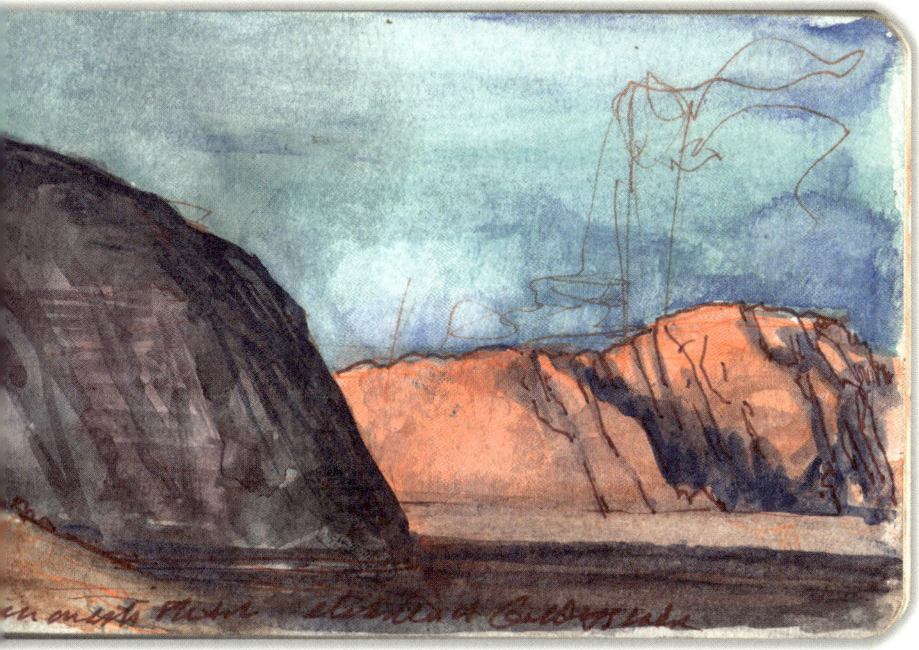

is accessible only to visitors accompanied by a licensed Navajo guide. Parking the Jeep, our guide led us to the edge of a conical mine tailing of gravel and rocky debris—remnants of the sandstone mass formerly occupying that space where now abides a gaping pothole arch. I estimated its height to be three or four stories above the valley floor. We decided to linger a while for lunch, which gave me some time to map out a composition and lay down some color notes. Never very talkative, our guide was more like an off-road-car service driver. He next delivered us to the Eye of the Sun, another pothole aperture atop a petrified bandshell that, in the failing light, was evocative of the installation art of James Turrell.

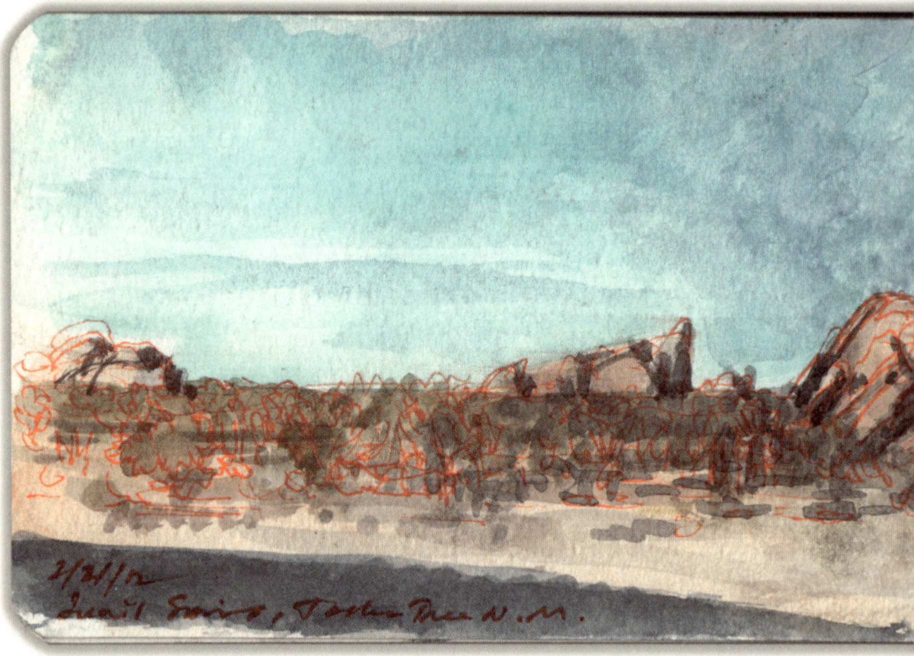

Fig. 23.

QUAIL SPRINGS, JOSHUA TREE NATIONAL PARK

Sliding east, the Pacific plate carried seawater beneath the North American plate. Combined with the heat generated by tectonic friction, superheated steam fractured overlying layers of sediment, allowing molten magma to rise through the fissures, filling gaps and caverns with hard igneous rock. As wind, water, and chemical erosion slowly removed the surrounding sedimentary rock, huge fantastical formations emerged, together with boulders larger than any glacial erratic. Rising suddenly from the desert floor, contiguous stony masses attract rock-face climbers, who gave them colorful names like Trashcan Rock, Ace of Spades, Baskerville Rock, and Popular Mechanics. These formations are located within the Quail Springs day-use area, accessible via the first turn-off and parking area approached from the

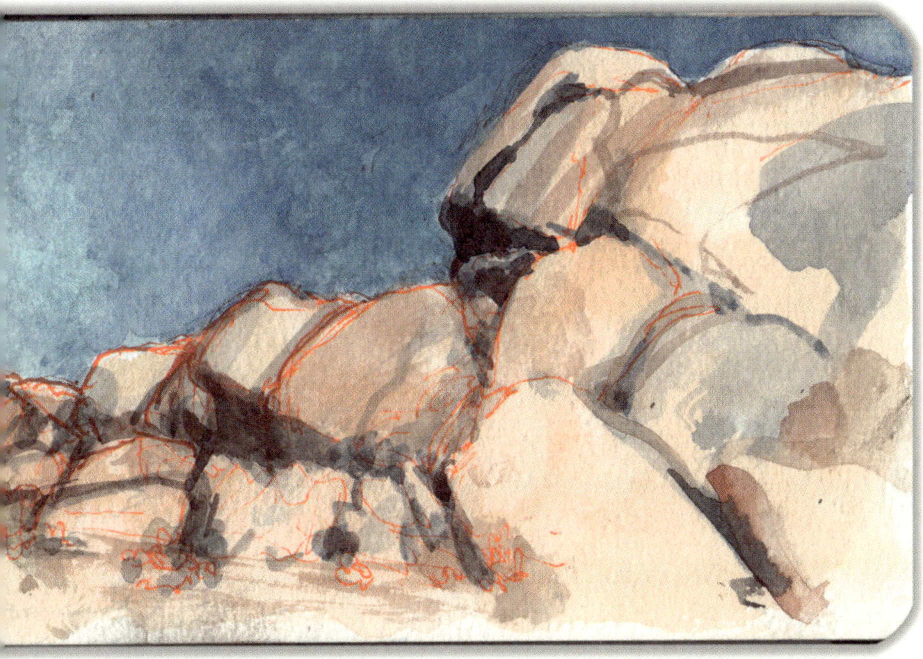

northeast portal of Joshua Tree National Park. The dramatic setting contrasts sharply with the almost level surface of the barren desert floor, punctuated by clumps of desperate vegetation and the eponymous Joshua tree, or Yucca brevifolia, which is not a tree but a kind of lily. Kathie and I paid our first visit to the site in advance of attending a professional conference in Los Angeles. Staying at a vintage motel, we were led by the dreadlocked manager into the garden and shown a makeshift shrine to his hero Gram Parsons. Following the twenty-six-year-old musician's death by overdose, his body was stolen from LAX by his friends and cremated in the Joshua Tree desert. When painting these subjects, one always faces the challenge of conveying a sense of scale, awe, and wonder.

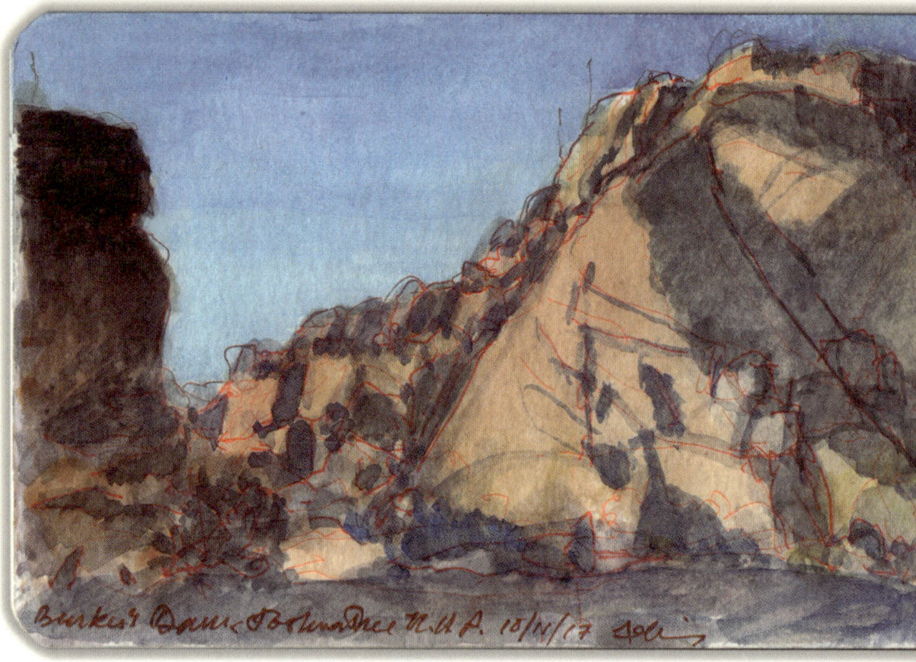

Fig. 24.

BARKER DAM, JOSHUA TREE NATIONAL PARK

Despite its remote location and inhospitable conditions, much of the terrain within Joshua Tree has accommodated human beings for thousands of years. Native American petroglyphs are scattered throughout the park. No physical remains have been found of permanent settlements, such as are common farther east within the Colorado, Gila, San Juan, and Rio Grande watersheds. During the late nineteenth century, geological formations such as Hidden Valley provided desperadoes with natural redoubts and enclosures for concealing stolen livestock. The rustler and counterfeiter Jim McHaney and his gang were later supplanted by legitimate cattlemen such as C. O. Barker, who built the first dam at this site to create a stock pond. Enlarged and improved in 1950 by the rancher Bill Keys and his wife, the barrier was

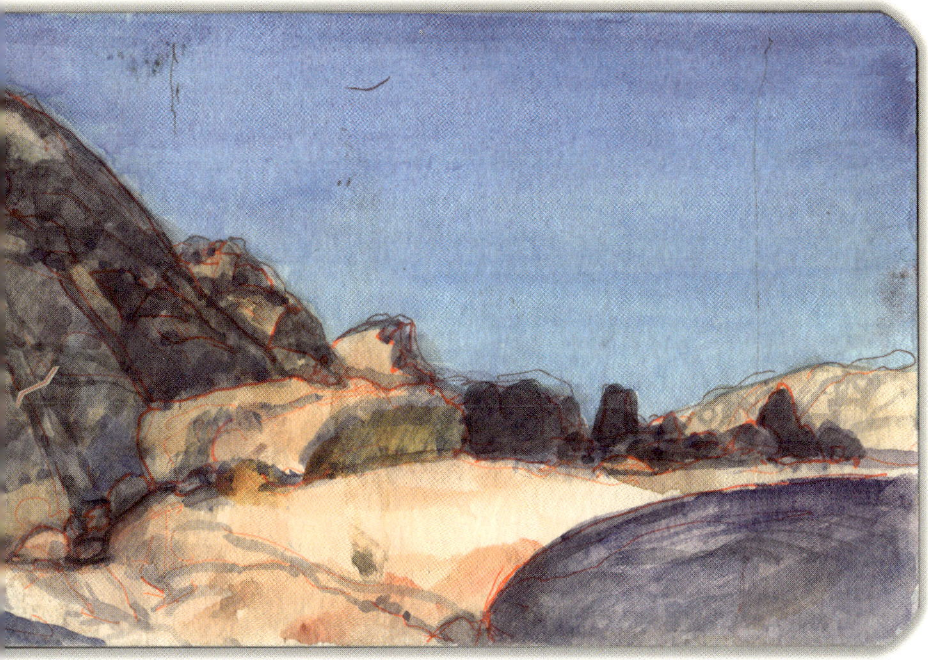

dubbed Big Horn Dam in honor of the wild sheep that shared the water with their herd. Approached along a well-marked trail, the newer concrete dam consists of upright slabs arranged in a zigzag pattern, reminiscent of stretches of the Berlin Wall. The adjoining area is a field of monzogranite. Smoothed by millions of years of erosion, the rectangular flat-topped boulders are deeply fissured. Some gaps are wide enough to walk through, others narrow enough to step across. On warm autumn days, one must take precautions to avoid lamentable encounters with dangerous creatures that still remain active. Dressed for the field in long pants and boots, I noted with amazement an astonishing number of visitors in shorts and flip-flops.

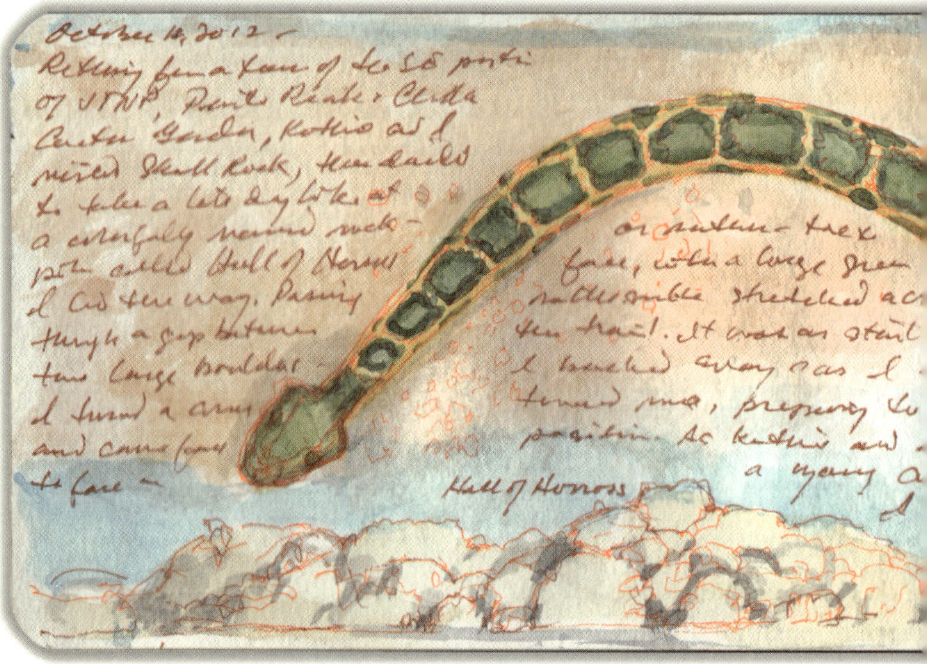

Fig. 25.

HALL OF HORRORS, JOSHUA TREE NATIONAL PARK

Heading south into the park from the town of Twentynine Palms, California, one passes striking rock formations with colorful names like Skull Rock and Hall of Horrors, where I had a run-in with a deadly Southern Pacific rattlesnake. Like its cousin the Mojave sidewinder, it has distinctive green-and-buff coloration. Taking note of each other, we parted without incident. As Kathie and I withdrew from the site, we warned a group of youths in light raiment wearing flip-flops and suntan lotion not to proceed. Scornful of the danger and the sage advice from their elders, they forged ahead. When we finally managed to get a cellphone signal, we called the visitor center to register our concern. A ranger answered. "We have seven venomous species in the park," he began. "The one you saw is one of the deadliest, with three

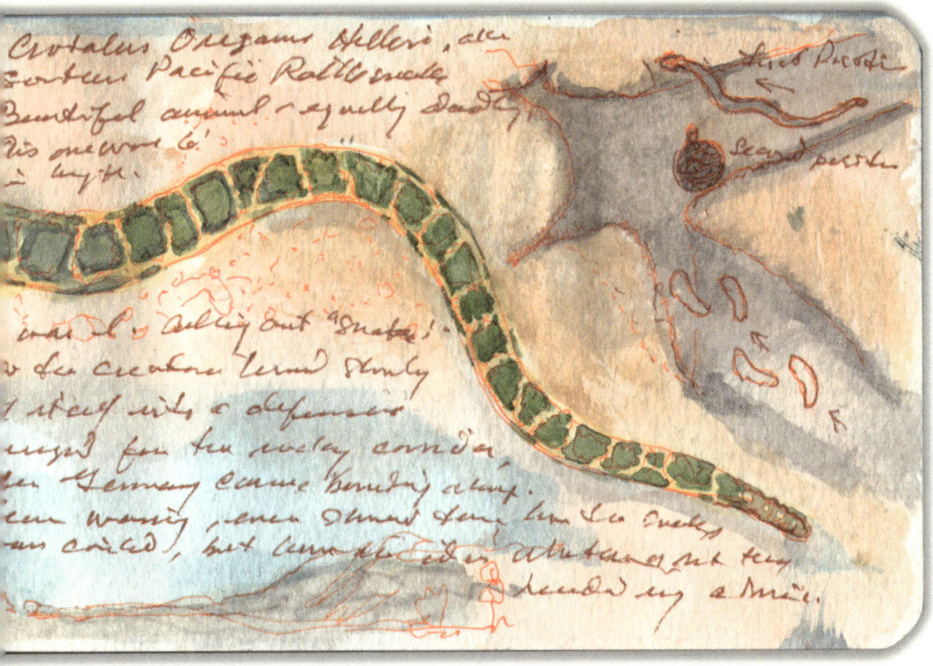

kinds of poison: a hemotoxin, neurotoxin, and powerful flesh-rotting digestive enzymes. Probably he was looking to score another meal before going into hibernation." We asked if many visitors get bitten each year, and the ranger replied, "Relatively few. Those who do usually provoked the creature or threatened it in some way. People lose dogs by letting them run off the leash in warmer seasons when snakes are active." The nearest hospital is in Yucca Valley, forty-five minutes from where we encountered the rattler. Cellphone reception exists within only a few miles of Twentynine Palms. In such an environment, mindfulness saves lives. My rendering of the snake was drawn from memory.

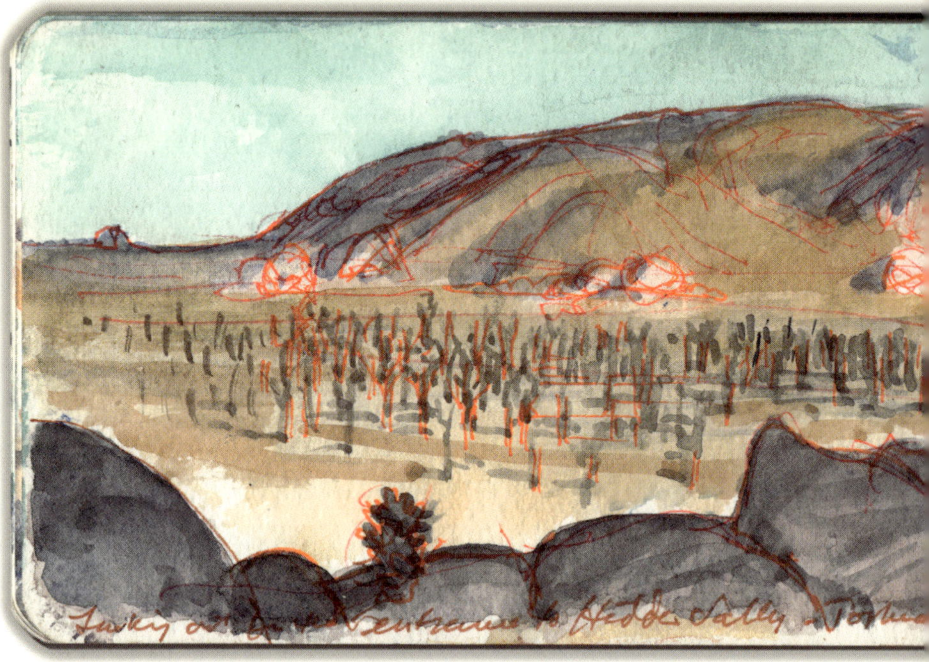

Fig. 26.

FROM THE ENTRANCE TO HIDDEN VALLEY,

Ascending (not descending) to the entrance of Hidden Valley, one beholds a sweeping vista stretching eastward across Lost Horse Valley toward Pinto Basin, past Ryan Mountain. Rising one thousand feet above the pediment, the summit, at 5,465 feet, is one of the highest points accessible to hikers within the park. The large, rocky outcropping to the right is classified an inselberg, or island mount, because it rises from the desert floor like an island in the sea. Known as pediment, the flat expanses between scattered elevations and outcroppings appear flat but are in fact slightly inclined. As wind, rain, and chemical erosion gnaw away at its slopes, the mountain retreats. The descending ground level forms a plain, exposing large gneiss formations to spheroid weathering. Entering through fissures created by

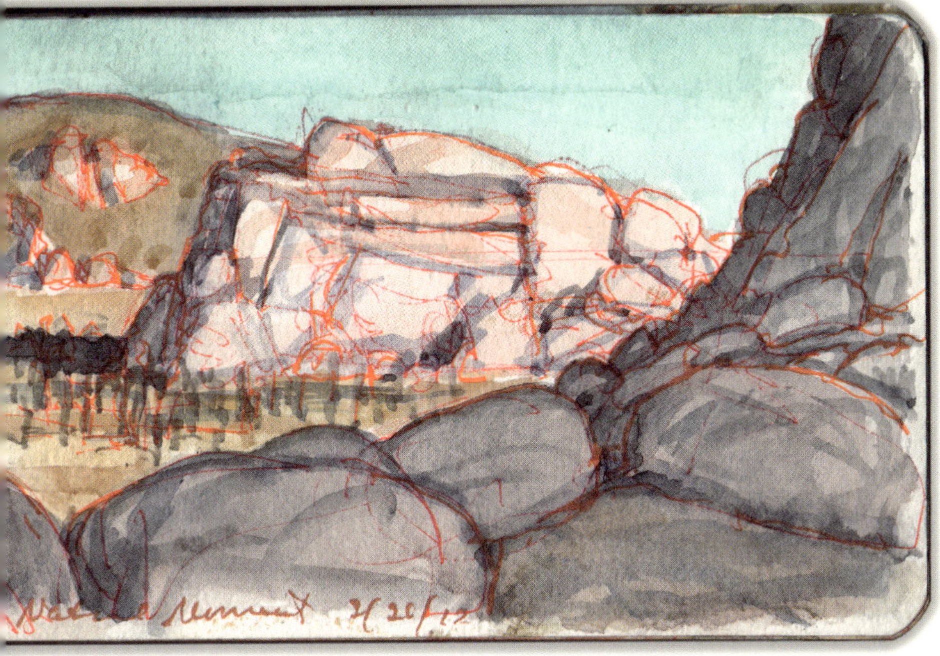

JOSHUA TREE NATIONAL PARK

immense pressure underground, water and chemicals cause erosion, together with windblown grit that sculpts the rock into organic forms. Scattered across the expanse between my perch and Ryan Mountain is an orderly grove of Joshua trees, Yucca brevifolia. In arranging this composition, it was important for me to capture geological variations: mountain, inselberg, pediment, and foliage. The image is framed with a shadowed foreground—a Claudian repoussoir substituting the rock wall to the right for an arboreal anchor. It was designed with a leftward diagonal sweep into the distance. Emerging from the close, almost intimate confines of the Hidden Valley Loop, I was delighted to be greeted by this panorama. Preserving that feeling is what I sought to convey.

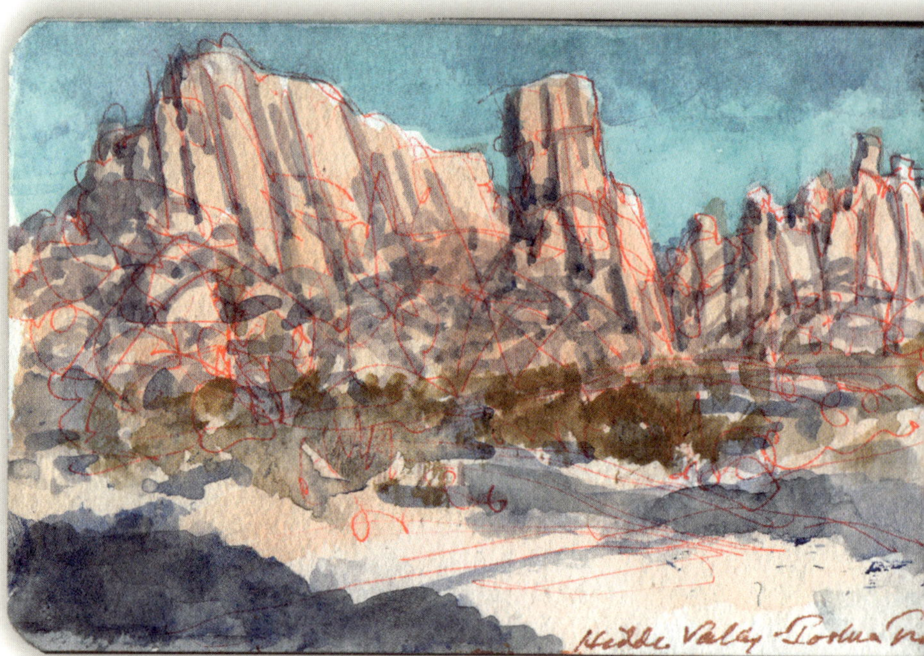

Fig. 27.

HIDDEN VALLEY, JOSHUA TREE NATIONAL PARK

Private efforts to preserve its unique setting and to protect a fragile ecosystem from real-estate development resulted in 825,000 acres being set aside as Joshua Tree National Monument in 1936. Forty years later, Congress protected 420,000 acres as wilderness. In 1994 Joshua Tree was promoted to park status. Naming the geological attractions in Joshua Tree National Park, like the buttes and arches in Monument Valley, was a way to bestow identity to recognizable features of terrain in ways that reflect a human desire for the picturesque. Skull Rock, Hall of Horrors, and Jumbo Rocks conjure up thrilling images of matinee adventures. Sculpted by tectonic activity and subsequent erosion, fantastical geological formations within the park have long served as a backdrop for television, cinema, and

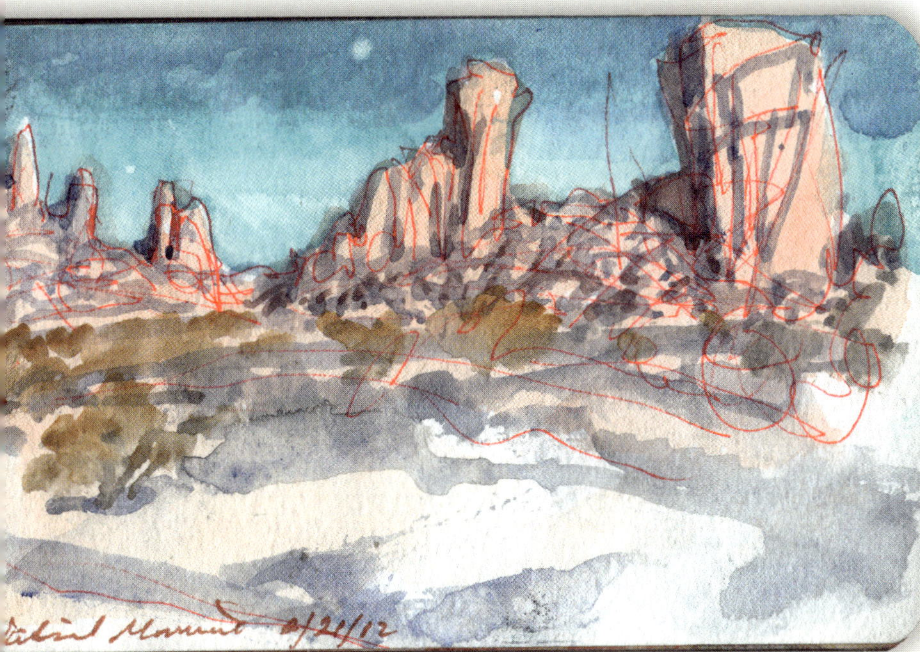

advertising photo shoots. Among these features is a semi-enclosed inselberg dubbed Hidden Valley. An easy mile-long loop trail and legendary escalades make Hidden Valley a magnet for rock-climbing enthusiasts. One remembers Chief Niwot's curse: beautiful places will attract so many people that their beauty will be lost. Sitting on a rock to produce this drawing, I was passed by dozens of hikers and a fair number of dogs. Many appeared to be late for a meeting, consuming the experience rather than absorbing it. The purpose of hikes is not to get to the finish line but to invite new experience. The words of John Burroughs came to mind: "If you want to learn something new, take the path you took yesterday."

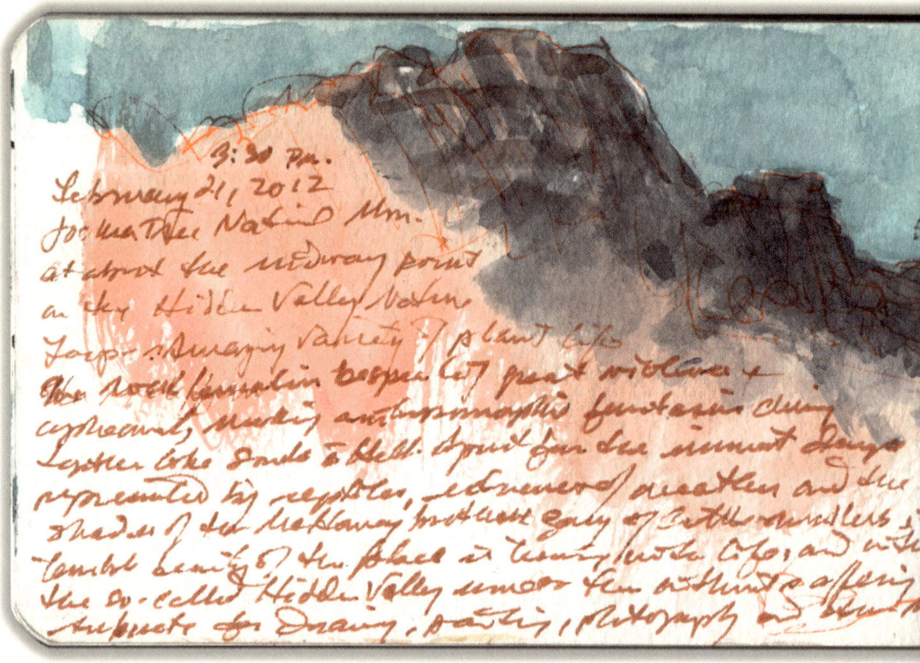

Fig. 28.

HIDDEN VALLEY, WITH FIELD NOTES

Drawing and writing are two sides of the same coin. Both are sensory-cognitive practices. One makes visible the spoken word, whereas the other transcribes visual sensation into written form. One finds in East Asian painting an almost effortless rapport between calligraphy and picture making, perhaps due in part to a writing system that has preserved some of its pictorial attributes. Remember the words of Rembrandt Peale: "Drawing is little else than writing the forms of objects." Expeditionary journal keeping is less about producing works of art than engaging an experience, digesting data, and compressing the file. The practice itself is the art. Always in the back of my mind is that Leonardo's greatest contribution is not the *Mona Lisa* but his sketchbooks.

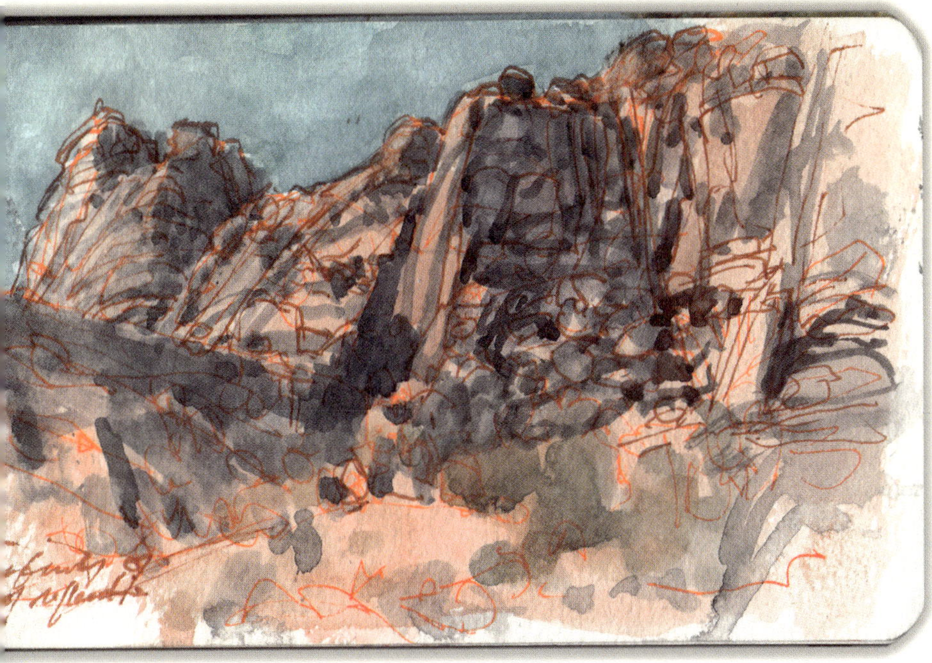

Written on the left side of this sketch is the following text:

> 3:30 PM February 21, 2012. Joshua Tree National Mon. at about the midpoint of the Hidden Valley Nature Loop—Amazing variety of plant-life. The rock formations bespeak of past violence + upheaval, making anthropomorphic fantasies clinging together like souls in Hell. Apart from the imminent danger represented by reptiles, inclement weather, and the shades of McHaney Brothers gang of cattle-rustlers, the terrible beauty of this place is teeming with life, and within the so-called Hidden Valley—some of them without (outside of Hidden Valley), offering an infinity of subjects for drawing, painting, photography, and other modes of reflection.

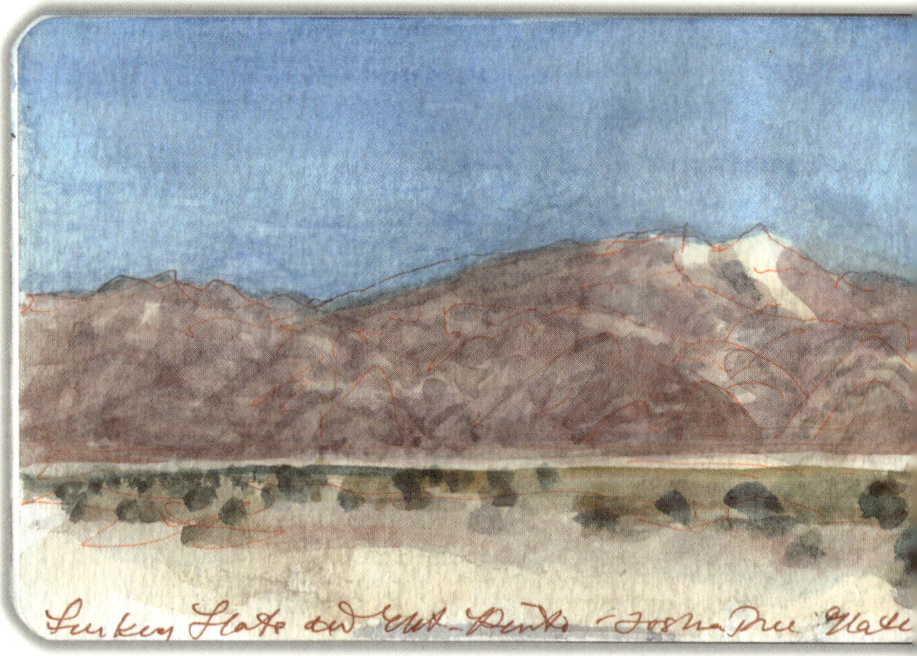

Fig. 29.

PINTO PEAK, JOSHUA TREE NATIONAL PARK

Joshua Tree National Monument sits atop a plateau where the Mojave Desert to the north meets the Sonoran Desert to the southeast. The park is named for the distinctive cactus known as the Joshua tree—*Yucca brevifolia* or, in Spanish, Izote de desierto. Otherworldly rock formations created by volcanism and erosion, cyclopean boulders, and outcroppings sculpted by erosion provide a perfect backdrop for westerns, science-fiction movies, and automobile commercials. Traveling southeast on the park road, one finds less abundant plant life before entering a scorched wasteland at the foot of the Hexie Mountains. En route to the Cottonwood Visitor Center is a large patch of fuzzy cholla cactus, dreaded by hikers for its flesh-stinging nettles. The

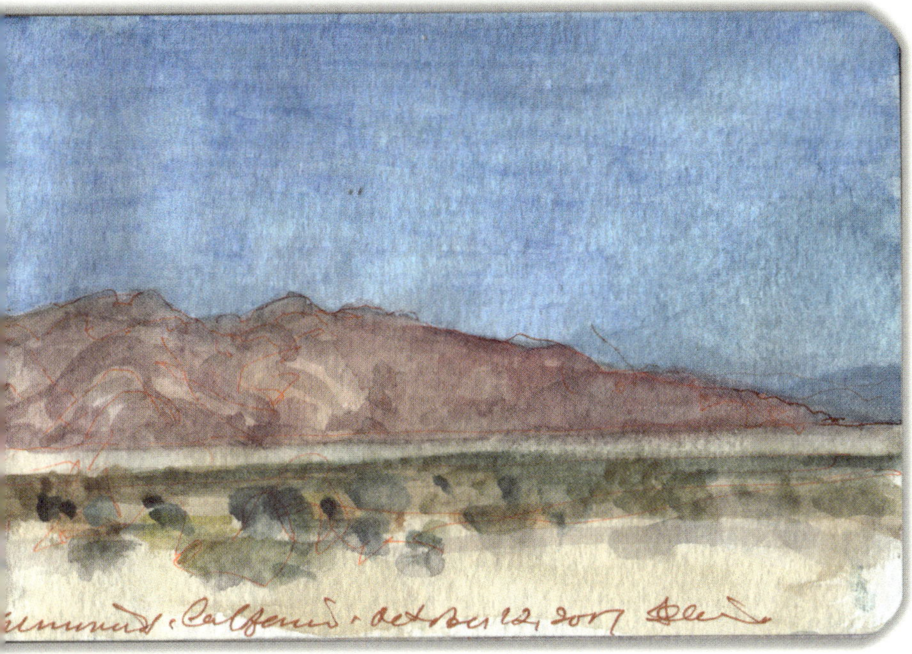

trail is well marked, with frequent cautions against touching the plants. On this October day, a small group of insouciant young women in party dresses and high heels ran among the cacti snapping selfies and othersies. As they gamboled among the cholla, a massive SUV arrived. Out of the vehicle stepped a large man in an evening gown, having a Priscilla, Queen of the Desert moment. Three male handlers and a female photographer followed him through the garden as he struck poses. His long diaphanous yellow scarf floated on light breezes, its selvage licking the nettles. Farther along Pinto Basin Road, a parking area faces a desolate plain. To the southeast, Pinto Mountain rises to an elevation of nearly five thousand feet.

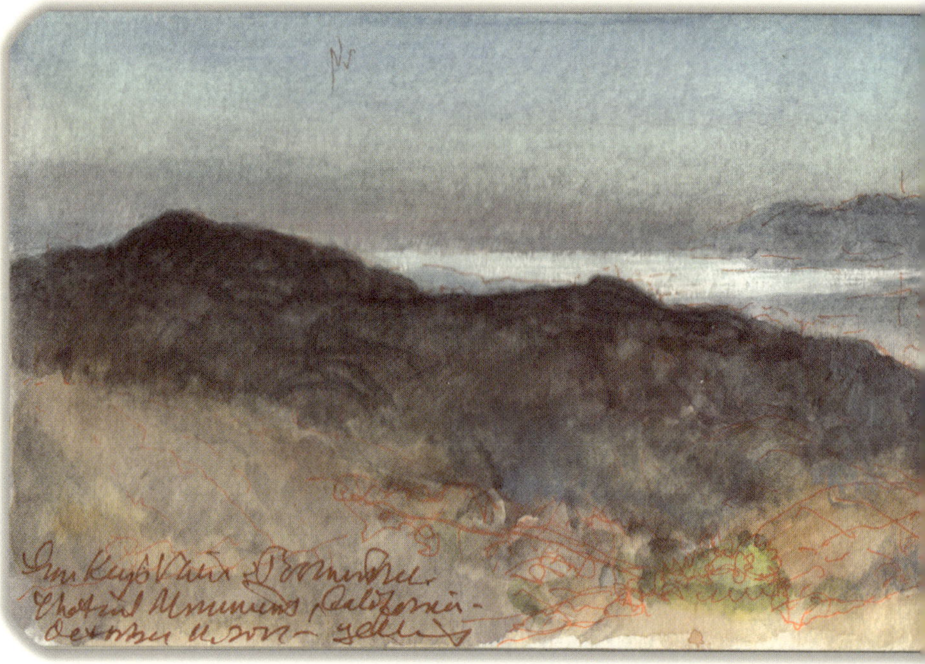

Fig. 30.

KEYS VIEW, JOSHUA TREE NATIONAL PARK

Throughout the park are scattered the ruins of played-out mines and failed farms. The Russian immigrant William F. Keys first came to Twentynine Palms to work in the Desert Queen Mine. He later filed a claim and established a ranch. His property is now located within the confines of the park. During a 1946 dispute, Keys shot and killed an interloper. Convicted for murder, he did eleven years at San Quentin before winning a pardon thanks to the efforts of the lawyer and Perry Mason mystery writer Erle Stanley Gardner. One of the park's frequently visited attractions is Keys View, a rocky promontory at the edge of the plateau, along the northern rim of Coachella Valley. Once the seabed of an inlet reaching up from the Sea of

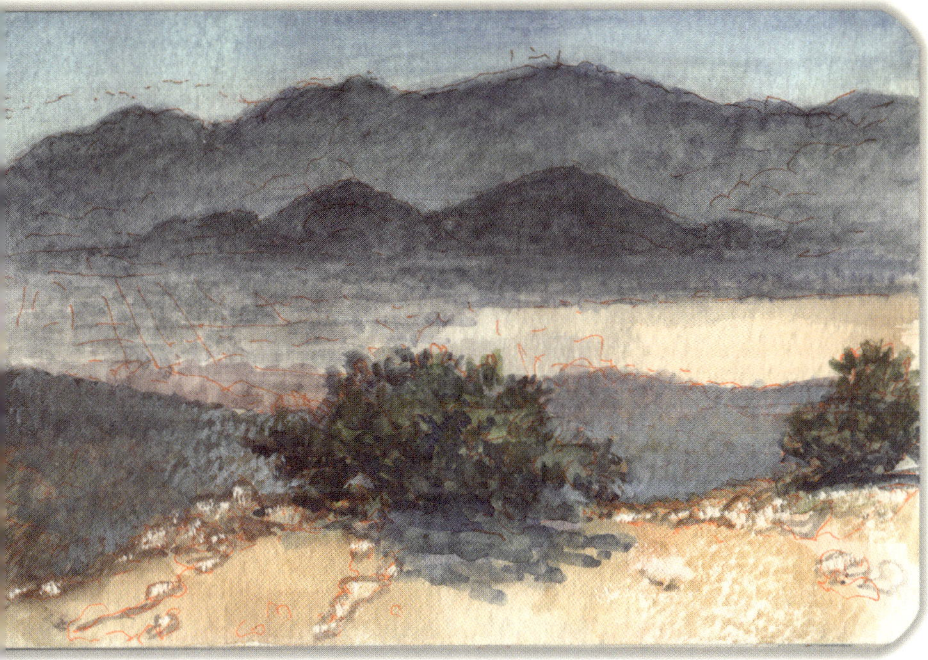

Cortez, the valley floor is a mile below the overlook, traversed longitudinally by a low ridge marking the San Andreas Fault. To the southeast lies the Salton Sea, 230 feet below sea level. Beyond that is the Imperial Valley, which once was part of the Colorado River watershed. Directly to the south are the San Jacinto Mountains. The eponymous peak has an elevation of just under 11,000 feet. Upscale communities including Palm Springs and Palm Desert spread out below its slopes. Hundreds of wind turbines rise from dry earth like skeletal dandelions. Their florets rotate majestically. A songbird landed in the piñon tree beside me. Wetting my brush, I touched the half-pan of ultramarine blue, wet it again, and began to paint.

Chapter 5

WORK PAGES

Bring a sketchbook outdoors. Add it to your daily routine. Write what you behold. Draw what you hear, whatever comes to mind. Alert to your surroundings, you should think of your personal field book as a handheld device powered only by mindfulness. Take a chance. Make a mark. Before producing a good drawing, one must first make a hundred bad ones, with the caveat that there are no bad drawings. There are only great drawings and research. Get busy. Take a trust fall. As John Burroughs said, “Leap, and the net will appear.”

It's just so beautiful. Everything.
—Maria Martinez

The health of the eye seems to demand a horizon. We are never tired, so long as we can see far enough.

—Ralph Waldo Emerson

We should talk less and draw more. Personally, I would like to renounce speech altogether and, like organic nature, communicate everything I have to say in sketches.
—Johann Wolfgang von Goethe

In a cold like this, the stars snap like distant coyotes, beyond the moon . . . and the place heaves with ghosts.

—D. H. Lawrence

An author knows his landscape best; he can stand around, smell the wind, get a feel for his place.
—Tony Hillerman

The sunshine in New Mexico could do almost anything. . . . It entered into one's deepest places and melted the thick, slow densities. It made one feel good. That is, alive.
—Mabel Dodge Luhan

We have an unknown distance yet to run, an unknown river to explore.

—John Wesley Powell

I don't believe in influence . . . in order to be an artist, you have to move. When you stop moving, then you're no longer an artist.
—Agnes Martin

If you would know the earth for what it really
is, learn it through its sacred places. . . .
You become one with a spirit that
pervades geologic time and space.
—N. Scott Momaday

Chapter 6

INTO THE FIELD

The American Southwest is a land of extremes. It is possible to wake up to a foot of snow on the ground and be playing golf or tennis in the afternoon. Mountaintops can exceed fourteen thousand feet while other areas, such as Death Valley and the Salton Sea, can descend to nearly three hundred feet below sea level. Seasonal changes in regions subject to blistering summer heat can deliver blizzard conditions in winter. Large expanses of the Southwest are sparsely inhabited, which can dangerously increase the response time to any kind of emergency. Similarly, cellphone service is limited and in some places nonexistent.

Never attempt off-road adventures in a conventional vehicle. Engage the services of qualified wilderness guides, such as whitewater rafting, fishing, and hunting outfitters. Even in public-use areas such as state and national parks, one might run afoul of wildlife like rattlesnakes or large mammals during mating season or with their young. Wherever you plan to go, do your homework, be fully prepared, make a plan, and keep to it.

MAKE A PLAN, KEEP TO A SCHEDULE

Prior to departing on a wilderness adventure, or even a day trip to an outdoor public-use area, make a plan. Calculate the driving time to and from your destination. Determine your route of march once you arrive and the duration of your visit. Leave the plan with a trusted friend or family member. Check in. Text or call them, if possible, when you arrive and when you depart. Should you become lost or suffer injury, law enforcement and emergency medical services will know where to effect your rescue. Make sure the available balance in your checking account or credit card will cover related costs. The tab for a helicopter rescue might be thousands of dollars. File a travel plan even if you will not be traveling alone. Carry phone numbers for EMS and law-enforcement agencies in case of emergency. Following these steps could save your life.

TRIBAL LANDS

Pueblos and tribal lands are semiautonomous administrative zones subject to federal authority. Upon entering these areas, one is no longer on state land and is thus subject to tribal law. Do your homework. Most of the pueblos and reservations have a website. Contact the visitor center for more information. A number of pueblos operate hotels and casinos. Native artists offer work for sale to the public, sometimes from shops attached to their homes. Some historic ruins and wilderness trails are under tribal authority. Do not stray from designated public areas. Be courteous and respectful. Behave like a guest. That is what you are.

MATERIALS AND EQUIPMENT

The mission of the sketchbook traveler is to devote as much time as possible to engaging with their surroundings, not struggling with bulky box easels, umbrellas, and any gear other than a small messenger bag or multi-pocket travel vest. Here are the essentials:

- Sketchbook
- Drawing tools
- Pocket paint box
- Travel brushes
- Water bottle for painting
- Bottle for drinking water
- Accessories: sponge, safety razor, beeswax stick, clips, folding pocket knife, compass, maps, camera and/or mobile phone, field glasses, etc.
- Multi-pocket travel vest
- Messenger bag or small knapsack to supplement carry capacity of the travel vest
- Insect repellent and sunscreen
- Folding tripod stool

DRESS FOR THE FIELD

Wear comfortable, practical clothing. Nineteenth-century artist-explorers wore the equivalent of hunting attire—a pullover frock coat, a wide-brimmed round hat for protection from the sun, a shirt and cravat that could double as a windbreaker scarf, and stout boots or high-quarter shoes worn with gaiters to cover the ankle. In period engravings, we can see artists wearing backpacks, onto which was strapped a collapsible umbrella that could be mounted on their walking sticks, along with a folding tripod stool.

Contemporary options are lighter and more portable. This book is addressed to anyone who wants to deepen and enrich their experience of travel through drawing and writing, not only to urban sketchers and plein-air painters, for which there exists a universe of paraphernalia. The following is focused specifically on outdoor garments and accessories for traveling light, on a sketchbook safari, carrying everything you might need on your person. Travelers visiting more settled areas like towns and cities can wear whatever street clothes suit their fancy, perhaps with the addition of a small shoulder bag or travel vest. Favor function over fashion, with the caveat that practical clothing has a style all its own. Please consult the list of suppliers at the back of this book.

- UV-PROOF AND INSECT-RESISTANT GARMENTS: Well-constructed long-sleeve cargo shirts and cargo trousers are recommended. A number of companies make clothing for fishermen that are permeated with insect repellent. In places where temperatures fluctuate greatly and rapid changes in weather are common, be sure to dress in layers.
- TRAVEL VEST: A wide array of options is available from a variety of suppliers. Look for strong construction and lots of pockets, including zippered inside security pockets. You will need to have room for a map, compass, sketchbook or journal, writing and drawing implements, a small watercolor box if you choose, travel brushes, sunglasses, camera, mobile phone, or both.
- HEADGEAR: A baseball cap offers less UV protection than a crushable, water-resistant, wide-brimmed round hat. A second option is an angler hat, some of which have larger bills and a neck drape to maximize coverage. A lightweight scarf or bandana can be useful for added protection.

- FOOTWEAR: Hiking boots are best for treks and trails. Urban explorers may want to acquire a good pair of walking shoes. I prefer sturdy oiled-leather ankle-high lace-up boots because they offer maximum lateral support and comfort. Everyone's feet are different. Finding the right fit will require some trial and error. Choose shoes that are appropriate to weather and terrain, with the correct sole tread, insulation, and waterproofing. Because you may be on your feet for hours at a time, comfort is a priority. I also recommend woolen and wool-blend socks for all seasons because they wick and emit fewer unpleasant odors after multiple days of wear. In areas frequented by venomous reptiles and stinging plants, long trousers layered with snake-proof chaps, gaiters, or boots are highly recommended.
- CLOTHING ACCESSORIES: In different settings and times of the year, you may want to invest in headgear with insect netting, snake-proof leggings, and a headlamp. I carry a pair of deerskin gloves in all four seasons, donning them only when necessary. Wearing gloves in winter deprives one's touch of the sensitivity required to write or paint outdoors. Instead, warm your hand inside a rag-wool sock, then push the butt end of the brush handle or pencil through a gap in the knitting. This technique allows you to work with bare fingers.
- INSECT REPELLENT AND SUNSCREEN: Research your destination. Learn what kinds of biting insects you wish to avoid. Mosquitoes and ticks can transmit unpleasant diseases to humans and animals. Use the appropriate repellent. If you are heading into the north woods or swimming in tropical waters, purchase bear and shark repellent. Likewise, use a maximum-strength sunscreen appropriate to the intensity of sunlight at your location.
- EMERGENCY PREPAREDNESS: Be sure to carry a standard first-aid kit along with anything else you might need to treat injuries that are possible in the terrain where you will be traveling, such as a Mylar survival blanket, butane lighter, fire starters, knife, walking stick, flashlight, compass, and maps. Take along a backup battery pack to recharge communication devices.

- WATER BOTTLE OR CANTEEN: No piece of equipment is more important. Staying hydrated is your top priority. I do not care for loose cylindrical water bottles, preferring instead to carry water in a more ergonomic nineteenth-century-style military canteen or contemporary hydration pack.
- FIELD BAG: A travel vest may replace your shoulder bag, or you may opt for extra storage to carry sketching materials, maps, books, compass, camera, and penknife.

WRITING AND DRAWING MATERIALS: SKETCHBOOKS

HAND-BOOK (Kansas City, Mo.). Global Art Hand-Book Journal (landscape format). Fine papers, but bindings can fail before the book is full of entries. Comparable in size to the pocket Moleskine watercolor sketchbook but thicker. Gusseted inside-cover back pocket.

MOLESKINE. Large selection. Strong bindings. The landscape-format watercolor sketchbooks contain archival paper of medium weight and quality. The pocket-sized journal (3.5 x 10 inches) is comparable in size to a mobile phone. Page spreads will fit on an A4 or 8 ½-by-11-inch flatbed scanner. Gusseted inside-cover back pocket.

PENTALIC. Aqua Watercolor Sketchbook Journal. Closer in size to the slimmer profile of the Moleskine journal. Produced by a well-known manufacturer of writing and calligraphy supplies.

STRATHMORE. Papers, drawing and watercolor journals.

WRITING AND DRAWING MATERIALS: TOOLS

KAWECO (Austria). Sport fountain or ballpoint pen. Hexagonal steel or brass body Sketch Up 56 technical pencil. Hexagonal steel or brass body Models also come in less durable plastic bodies at lower prices.

PILOT (Japan). Full selection of fine and technical writing instruments

ROTRING (Germany). Full selection of fine and technical writing instruments

SAKURA MICRON (Japan). Archival waterproof ink. Wonderful for use with ink wash and watercolors. A disposable version of a rapidiograph pen. Sold in black and a wide array of colors and point widths.

BRUSHES

DA VINCI (Germany) Travel brushes
ESCODA (Spain) Travel brushes
RICHESON (US) Plein-air watercolor brush set

WATERCOLORS

DIXON TICONDEROGA
US importer of Maimeri watercolors (Italy) and distributor of Canson and Strathmore papers and sketchbooks. Not a retail source. Contact your local art-supply store.
GOLDEN (US)
The gold standard in acrylic colors, Golden has developed the new QoR line of watercolors using synthetic resin in place of Gum-Arabic: https://www.qorcolors.com
KREMER PIGMENTE (Germany and US)
Selection of travel sets and related materials. Online and walk-in retail sales.
L. CORNELISSEN & SON (UK)
Full selection of pans, tubes, and related materials. Retail walk-in and online sales.
SCHMINCKE (Germany)
Full selection of related materials. Contact your local art-supply store.
SENNELIER (France)
Full selection of related materials. Retail outlet in Paris and online. Contact your local art-supply store
WINSOR & NEWTON (UK and US)
Full selection. Contact your local art-supply store.

LOCAL ART SUPPLIES

ARIZONA ART SUPPLY, Phoenix: https://www.arizonaartsupply.com
ARTISAN, Santa Fe: https://www.artisansantafe.com
H. R. MEININGER ART MATERIAL, Denver: https://www.meininger.com
TAOS ART SUPPLY: https://www.facebook.com/taosartsupply

BAGS AND SATCHELS

FILSON: Small and medium field bags
FROST RIVER: Field Satchel, small
L. CORNELISSEN & SON: Leather Artists Sketch Bag
ORVIS: Safe Passage sling pack

MISCELLANEOUS

WALKSTOOL: Swedish-made telescoping tripod stool in carry bag
REI: Co-op Trail Stool. Fixed legs with carry strap

GENERAL OUTDOOR CLOTHING—HIKING AND CAMPING

FILSON: General line of outdoor clothing and field bags
DULUTH TRADING COMPANY: Travel vests, cargo pants, shoulder bags, and day packs
FROST RIVER TRADING COMPANY: Large assortment of shoulder bags and backpacks
L.L. BEAN: General line of outdoor clothing
ORVIS: General line of outdoor clothing
PATAGONIA: General line of outdoor clothing
REI: General line of outdoor clothing
TILLEY (Canada): Travel vest and hats

OUTDOOR FOOTWEAR

CHIPPEWA: Snake-proof boots and hunting boots
DANNER: Hiking boots
FRYE BOOT COMPANY: Various styles
RED WING: Heritage Collection and hiking boots
S.A.S. (San Antonio Shoe Co.): Daily footwear
WOLVERINE: Thousand-Mile Boots

Chapter 7

ORGANIZATIONS AND INSTITUTIONS

Georgia O'Keeffe Museum, Santa Fe
www.okeeffemuseum.org

Ghost Ranch, Abiquiu
www.ghostranch.org

Great Prairie Highway, Santa Fe Trail
www.nps.gov/safe/index.htm

Harwood Museum, Taos
taos.org/what-to-do/arts-culture/museums

Historic Route 66
www.historic66.com

Mabel Dodge Luhan House, Taos
www.mabeldodgeluhan.com

Millicent Rogers Museum, Taos
millicentrogers.org

Museum of Indian Arts & Culture, Santa Fe
miaclab.org

New Mexico History Museum, Santa Fe
www.nmhistorymuseum.org

New Mexico Museum of Art, Santa Fe
nmartmuseum.org

New Mexico Museum of Natural History and Science, Albuquerque
nmnaturalhistory.org

Northern Rio Grande National Heritage Area, Española
www.riograndenha.org

Palace of the Governors, Santa Fe
www.palaceofthegovernors.org

Taos Art Museum at Fechin House
www.taosartmuseum.org

Chapter 8

PARKS, OPEN SPACES, AND DESTINATIONS

It would take a lifetime to explore the Southwestern United States. These are some of the places I have visited over the years. Many have a connection with my work or with historic events and expeditions or the literature included in the chapter 9 reading list.

Acoma Pueblo
www.puebloofacoma.org

Bandelier National Monument
www.nps.gov/band/index.htm

Bent's Old Fort National Historic Site
www.nps.gov/beol/index.htm

Canyon de Chelly National Monument
www.nps.gov/cach/index.htm

Chaco Culture National Historical Park
www.nps.gov/chcu/index.htm

Cochiti Pueblo
www.newmexico.org/places-to-visit/native-culture/cochiti-pueblo

Coronado Historic Site
nmhistoricsites.org/coronado

D. H. Lawrence Ranch
dhlawrenceranch.unm.edu/d.h.-lawrence-ranch/index.html

El Camino Real de Tierra Adentro National Historic Trail
www.nps.gov/elca/index.htm

El Morro National Monument
www.nps.gov/elmo/index.htm

Ernest Blumenschein House, Taos
www.taoshistoricmuseums.org

Fort Union National Monument
www.nps.gov/foun/index.htm

Francisco Fort Museum
www.franciscofort.org

Georgia O'Keeffe House and Welcome Center
www.okeeffemuseum.org/home-and-studio

Glorieta Battlefield
www.battlefields.org/visit/battlefields/glorieta-pass-battlefield

Great Sand Dunes National Park & Preserve
www.nps.gov/grsa/index.htm

Hubbell Trading-Post
www.nps.gov/hutr/planyourvisit/auction.htm

Joshua Tree National Park
www.nps.gov/jotr/index.htm

Mesa Verde National Park
www.nps.gov/meve/index.htm

Monument Valley Tribal Park
navajonationparks.org/tribal-parks/monument-valley

Orilla Verde Recreation Area
www.blm.gov/visit/orilla-verde-recreation-area

Pecos National Historical Park
www.nps.gov/peco/index.htm

Petroglyph National Monument
www.nps.gov/petr/index.htm

Puye Cliff Dwellings
www.puyecliffdwellings.com

Sanctuario de Santo Niño de Atocha de Chimayo
www.holychimayo.us

Taos Pueblo
taospueblo.com

Valles Caldera National Preserve
www.nps.gov/vall/index.htm

White Rock Canyon
visitlosalamos.org/wpcontent/uploads/2020/06/White_Rock_Canyon.pdf

Wild Rivers State Recreation Area
www.blm.gov/visit/wild-rivers-recreation-area

Chapter 9

READING LIST

A note to the reader: Below is a list of special-interest books one is unlikely to find at every bookstore or visitor center. Some are available online. Others may be requested through interlibrary loan. Some have been made available as free downloads, such as from Gutenberg.org, or as print-on-demand facsimile editions. You are encouraged to follow your own interest, whether that be hiking, angling, or camping or science, history, or art. All these narratives are intertwined. Follow the path that rises to your feet. When stopping to rest, have something great to read.

Abbey, Edward. *Desert Solitaire*. New York: Random House, 1968.

Broder, Patricia Janis. *Taos: A Painter's Dream*. New York: New York Graphic Society, 1980.

Cabeza de Vaca, Álvar Núñez. *The Narrative of Cabeza de Vaca*. Reprint. Lincoln: University of Nebraska Press, 2003.

Cantú, Francisco. *The Line Becomes a River: Dispatches from the Border*. New York: Riverhead Books, 2018.

Cather, Willa. *Death Comes for the Archbishop*. New York: A. A. Knopf, 1927.

Cushing, Frank Hamilton. *The Correspondence and Journals of Frank Hamilton Cushing, 1879–1884*. Edited by Jesse Green. Albuquerque: University of New Mexico Press, 1990.

Flint, Richard, and Shirley Cushing Flint. *The Coronado Expedition, from the Distance of 460 Years*. Albuquerque: University of New Mexico Press, 2012.

Haika, Chronic. *Roadside Geology of New Mexico*. Missoula, MT: Mountain Press, 1987.

Hall, Dawn, ed. *Drawing the Borderline: Artist-Explorers of the U.S.–Mexico Boundary Survey*. Albuquerque, NM: Albuquerque Museum, 1996.

Hart, Stephen Harding, and Archer Butler Hulbert, eds. *The Southwestern Journals of Zebulon Pike, 1806–1807*. Albuquerque: University of New Mexico Press, 2006.

Hillerman, Tony. *The Spell of New Mexico*. Albuquerque: University of New Mexico Press, 1976.

Hine, Edward. *Edward Kern and the American Expansion*. New Haven: Yale University Press, 1962.

Horgan, Paul. *Great River: The Rio Grande in American History*. New York: Rinehart & Co., 1954.

Magoffin, Susan Shelby. *Down the Santa Fe Trail and into Mexico: The Diary of Susan Magoffin, 1846–1847*. Edited by Stella M. Drumm, introduction by Howard R. Lamar. 1926. Reprint, Lincoln: University of Nebraska, 1982.

McPhee, John. *Rising from the Plains*. New York: Farrar, Straus & Giroux, 1987.

Momaday, N. Scott. *Man Made of Words: Essays, Stories, Passages*. New York: St. Martin's Griffin, 1998.

Morand, Anne. *Thomas Moran: The Field Sketches, 1856–1923*. Tulsa: University of Oklahoma Press, 1995.

Nichols, John. *New Mexico Trilogy: The Nirvana Blues, The Magic Journey, The Milagro Beanfield War.* New York: Ballantine, 1987.

Poole, Joy L., ed. *Over the Santa Fe Trail to Mexico: The Travel Diaries and Autobiography of Dr. Rowland Willard.* Norman: University of Oklahoma Press, 2005.

Powell, John Wesley. *The Exploration of the Colorado River and Its Canyons.* New York: Penguin Books, 2003.

Sides, Hampton. *Blood and Thunder: The Epic Story of Kit Carson and the Conquest of the American West.* New York: Doubleday, 2007.

Simpson, Lieutenant James H. *Navaho Expedition: Journal of a Military Reconnaissance from Santa Fe, New Mexico to the Navaho Country, Made in 1849.* Norman: University of Oklahoma Press, 2003.

Solnit, Rebecca. *Drowned River: The Death and Rebirth of Glen Canyon on the Colorado.* Santa Fe, NM: Radius Books, 2018.

Stillman, Deanne, with Galen Hunt (photographer). *Joshua Tree: Desolation Tango* (Desert Places). Tucson: University of Arizona Press, 2006.

Streit, Taylor. *Fly Fishing New Mexico. No Nonsense Guides.* London: Facet Publishing, 2004.

Walker, Lawrence R., and Frederick H. Landau. *A Natural History of the Mojave Desert.* Tucson: University of Arizona Press, 2016.

Water, Frank. *Book of the Hopi.* New York: Viking, 1963.

Webster, David J. *Richard Kern: Expeditionary Artist in the Far Southwest, 1848–1853.* Fort Worth, TX: Amon Carter Museum, 1985.

ACKNOWLEDGMENTS

Pete Schiffer, Joc Langman, Sandra Korinchak, Peggy Kellar, and the entire crew at the Schiffer Book Farm in Atglen, Pennsylvania, have outdone themselves in the creation of this book. I could not be more delighted with the result. For their friendship, support and hospitality, I am profoundly grateful to Dr. Sigmund Jenssen and Mollie Bolger Jenssen. Many thanks to trusted éditrice par excellence Pamela Barr, for her patience and guidance in shaping these texts. I am also deeply grateful to Maria Hajic, Evan Feldman, and John Macker at Gerald Peters Gallery in Santa Fe for believing in my work, and to Don Stinson for his friendship over the years and for putting us all together. Thanks also to Mark Golden of Golden Artist Colors, inc. and to Philip Garrett for their generous technical support; and to master printers Mike Costello of Hand Graphics in Santa Fe and Cindi Royce Ettinger in Philadelphia for helping to expand my artistic practice, along with Thomas Park at Orion Studios in Santa Fe. Numerous other artists, friends, and new acquaintances whose input and guidance proved valuable include, David Chickey of Radius Books, Vicki Davila and Ted Stanley, Vivian George and Shane Murphy, Sandy Goins, Bill Havu, Edgar and Shanna Heap of Birds, Ylise Kessler, Anne Lewis and Francis Flotron, Marcia Nebera, Nick Ryan, Mike Taylor, and Patricia Lea Watts of Ecoartspace. Most of all, I will be forever and eternally indebted to my loving spouse, secret weapon, and guiding light, Kathie Manthorne.

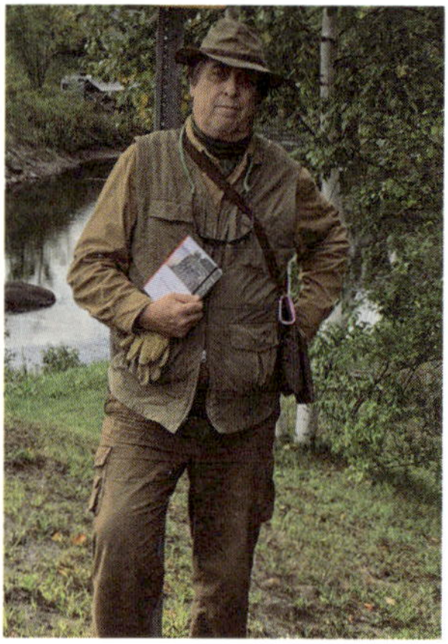

ABOUT THE AUTHOR

James Lancel McElhinney is a visual artist, author, and essayist known for travel journals and other works exploring American rivers and Civil War landscapes. Exhibited widely, McElhinney earned a BFA from Tyler School of Art and MFA from Yale, and he is the recipient of grants from the Pollock-Krasner Foundation Grant and the National Endowment for the Arts. His art is represented in many public and private collections, including the Denver Art Museum and the Museum of the Southwest. McElhinney lives in Manhattan and the Champlain Valley with his wife, the scholar and author Dr. Katherine E. Manthorne. Learn more at *mcelhinneyart.com*.